The Songs of
DOC WATSON

The Songs of

DOC WATSON

OAK PUBLICATIONS
New York • London • Sydney

Photographs:

Cover and book design by Jean Hammons
Cover Photograph by Dan Seeger

Copyright © 1971 by Oak Publications,
A Division of Embassy Music Corporation, New York
All Rights Reserved

Order No. OK 62489
International Standard Book Number: 0.8256.0120.7
Library of Congress Catalog Card Number: 70-113475

Exclusive Distributors:
Music Sales Corporation
257 Park Avenue South, New York, NY 10010 USA
Music Sales Limited
8/9 Frith Street, London W1V 5TZ England
Music Sales Pty. Limited
120 Rothschild Street, Rosebery, Sydney, NSW 2018, Australia

Printed in the United States of America by
Vicks Lithograph and Printing, Inc.

Contents

Introduction

Let me think about music for a minute. My first introduction to music came from my memory of being held in my mother's arms very comfortably. I remember the feeling was very warm and the sound was like that of *The Lone Pilgrim* being harmonized by the congregation. From my very early childhood on, I can remember my mother singing. She'd sing around the house while churning butter, or while patching some of dad's overalls that he'd worn the life out of. My dad didn't play around the house too much. He was a pretty serious fellow and devoted most of his evenings to trying to see that we got enough of the word of God so that we knew the Golden Rule and the way to live morally decent lives, and that we knew some of the songs so that we could sing along when he took us to church. Both of my parents worked very hard to keep us from starving; there were eleven of us in the family, and it was right during the depression.

I used to play with everything that had a musical sound around the house. I must have been a real pest to my mother. Every Christmas, just as far back as I can remember, Santa Claus slipped a harmonica in the big old stocking that I'd get to hang up on the mantle piece. That was my first introduction to a musical instrument. I could play tunes on the harmonica pretty well, even before I could note a single tune on the banjo.

My brother Arnold played the banjo at home, and every once in a while my father would pick a few tunes. One day Dad told me, "You know, I believe you could learn to play a banjo, son. I've a good mind to make you one." That was along in the winter when he said that, and the next summer he came in with some pieces for a five-string. He made a round maple hoop, managed to find some tension hooks, and made it so that the head part looked a little like a *no'the'n* banjo, or one that was built in a factory.

I started playing the guitar a little when my first cousin left his guitar at our house for a while; also, I had learned a few chords from an old boy at school who played the guitar. I was messing with my cousin's guitar one morning before Dad went to work, and he turned around to me after he had finished his breakfast and said, "Now, son, if you learn to play just one little tune on that by the time I get back, we'll go to town Saturday and buy you a guitar." Well, I knew I had him right there, because I knew almost enough already to play a song, and I knew that I could be singing along with my playing by the time he got back. The first song I learned on the guitar was *When The Roses Bloom In Dixieland* by the Carter Family. My dad was just as good as his word; we went to town and found me a little guitar. It was one of those ten dollar guitars—a pretty good little thing to learn on, but as hard to fret as a barbed wire fence. A few years later, when I was sixteen or seventeen, I earned enough money from cutting down some dead chestnut extract timber (used for tanning leather) to order a guitar from Sears and Roebuck.

While I learned a lot of music from my family and the people who lived near us, I also learned a great deal of music from records. Dad worked a week at the sawmill and bought a little wind-up graphophone and fifty or sixty records from my uncle, who had decided to buy a bigger one. There was everything from Jimmie Rodgers to the Carter Family, Gid Tanner and the Skillet Lickers, and John Hurt. When I started to play the guitar I listened especially to records of these people and others, including, of course, the Delmore Brothers, and later on, Merle Travis. I knew hardly any of the recording stars personally. I did know Clarence Ashley and Garley Foster, though. I never had the pleasure of meeting Jimmie Rodgers, and I'm sorry to say that I never met Uncle Dave Macon. I loved his records with all the fun and foolishness he did in his singing. I've met Maybelle and Sarah Carter since I've grown up, but back then I didn't know them. When you hear the music of a lot of those people, though, not just one or two songs but a variety of things, you realize when you meet them that you already know them through their music.

I began to be influenced by other music when I went to school. I heard old records from the collections of some of the teachers at Raleigh—records of musicians like Nick Lucas and Django Reinhardt, as well as the big jazz bands. Old-time country music is not the only kind of music I ever heard. I worked ten years with a country swing group headed up by a friend of mine, Jack Williams. In that band I learned quite a few of the old pop standards—not the way they are written on sheet music, but country versions of them.

About the time I was eighteen, the name "Doc" happened. I was doing a remote control radio show from a furniture store in Lenoire, North Carolina. The young man I worked with played the guitar and sang some, and his name was Paul Greer; they called him Paul, which was nice and short over the radio. The announcer came to me before we were on the air and said, "Your name's Arthel." He pronounced it kind of slow and said, "That's too long. What's a good short name for the radio? Let's think up a good name right here." There was a young lady there—she must have been fourteen or fifteen—and she yelled out, "Call him 'Doc' ". I never found out who she was; she was just back in the audience in the furniture store. The name "Doc" has come in very handy to me as a professional name because it's easy to remember.

I play the guitar because I love it better than any other instrument that I could ever hope to learn how to play. When I play a song, be it on the guitar or banjo, I live that song, whether it is a happy song or a sad song. Music, as a whole, expresses many things to me—everything from beautiful scenery to the tragedies and joys of life. If I feel good, I play music to expend energy. It's a good way, a happy way, of getting enjoyment out of releasing some energy. Sometimes, too, if I'm under tension, and I've got a guitar and a good song on my mind, first thing I know, I'm relaxed again. Whether I'm playing just for myself or for an enthusiastic audience, I can get the same emotions I had when I found that Dad had seen to it that Santa Claus brought exactly what I wanted for Christmas. A true entertainer, I think, doesn't ever lose that feeling.

Doc Watson

Doc's introduction and notes on the songs were edited by Ron Stanford from his interviews with Doc at Deep Gap, North Carolina in August, 1970.

Doc Watson

Western North Carolina has long been recognized as one of the richest repositories of folk song and lore in the southeastern United States.

On his first visit to the southern mountains in 1916, Cecil Sharp initiated his collecting activities in the six western-most counties of this state. In the total of his three visits to this country, he collected more tunes in North Carolina than in any other state, though he spent a bit more time in Kentucky. Maud Karpeles, in her preface to the second edition of "English Folk Songs from the Southern Appalachians," remarks that "the most fertile ground was on either side of the big mountain range known as the Great Divide, which separates the states of North Carolina and Tennessee."

Just below the crest of this eastern continental divide, some thirty-three hundred feet up in the mountains, is the Deep Gap community, home of Doc Watson and family. Here, in some of the south's most beautiful and still unspoiled expanse of mountainous terrain, Doc was born in 1923. From infancy he lived with music in the air around him, and being blind from birth he heard it all the more keenly. Some of the songs and ballads which he sings today are those which his mother used when lulling her children to sleep: *The House Carpenter, Katie Mory, Wreck On The C&O*, to mention a few.

The family gathered nightly before bedtime to read a chapter from the Bible and sing a few hymns from the "Christian Harmony," the post-Civil War hymnal which, from 1866 until the late 1920s, found its way into more mountain homes than any other collection of sacred music.

The instrumental music came after Doc had sung for a few of his childhood years. From about the time he was six onwards, a new harmonica was tucked into every Christmas stocking, and from his dad Doc learned to play the local fiddle tunes and breakdowns. General Watson (a Christian name rather than military rank) crafted a homemade banjo with a groundhog hide for a skin when Doc was about ten years old and this was the boy's first fretted instrument. The banjo technique he also acquired from his father's musical examples and later from his brother Arnold's.

The family had, by this time, purchased an old, wind-up phonograph along with a supply of early country music recordings. The sounds of Gid Tanner and the Skillet Lickers, Al Hopkins and the Buckle Busters, Riley Puckett and the Carter Family were blended with those of local fiddlers, guitar and banjo pickers and family singers to broaden Doc's musical horizons.

It was not until two years after he had entered the Raleigh School for the Blind that Doc obtained a guitar. The first tune he learned was *When The Roses Bloom In Dixieland*, as played by Maybelle Carter on the original Carter Family recording; techniques were easily acquired on the guitar, and Doc soon realized that this was his instrument.

Having been educated in a comparatively large, urban center, Doc was continually exposed to classical music during his years at school, and being unusually sensitive to music of all kinds, he absorbed a great deal from this exposure. He developed a more sophisticated concept of harmony than he would have had if he had gone to school in the mountains, and this process was furthered by his participation, some years later, in a "rock-a-billy" combo. It would have been interesting indeed to hear the music Doc might have played had his musical education been confined to the vocal and instrumental music of the area around his home. Given these musical limitations and such talent as Doc possesses, one might speculate that his inventive musical genius might have led him to create new tunes or ways of playing other instruments. Instead, the broadening of his harmonic conception has enabled him to experiment with many different types of music, adapting not only the highly ornamented mountain fiddle tunes to his style of flat picking, but such old pop dance favorites as *The Sheik of Araby, Whispering* and simple airs often associated with beginner's courses for the piano, such as *Country Gardens*.

In short, Doc does not share the folklorist's musical prejudices; he will often joke about ruining his "image" and then go ahead and play one of those "anything but a folk song" tunes on the guitar.

Although he did not complete his formal education, Doc has continued to study through the facilities of "talking books" supplied to blind persons throughout the U.S. by the Library of Congress. His fund of knowledge, both theoretical and practical, in the field of electronics would qualify him for a well-paid position if he were not blind, and he has often said that given his sight he would probably never have developed his musical talents to the degree that he has, but would rather have studied electrical engineering.

Although he was born and raised in prime folk song territory and had music in the family, Doc is by no means a representative of the vocal or instrumental music of his area. He was born too late to develop a strongly regional-personal style, for within three months of his birth date, Fiddlin' John Carson recorded the first "hillbilly" disc, and within two years the Grand Ole Opry was launched in Nashville by Fiddlin' Uncle Jimmy Thompson. Through radio and phonograph records, Doc was introduced to a wide variety of regional folk styles and repertoires at an early age. He cannot, for example, be said to characterize the western North Carolina singing or instrumental style in the same way that Roscoe Holcomb represents the "high, lonesome sound" so typical of eastern Kentucky.

Doc's basic repertoire and instrumental styles are directly reflective of the three main musical influences of his childhood: (1) sacred and secular music learned from family and neighbors; (2) phonograph records heard from early childhood; (3) songs and dance tunes learned from the radio performances of such folk professionals as Uncle Dave Macon, the Monroe and the Delmore Brothers, and Merle Travis, to mention a few. Doc then is a musical hybrid, but a hybrid of a very special sort. His sensitivity to style was at work from his earliest years as a musican. Thus, he had, without consciously attempting to reproduce the performance of another musician, retained the spirit of the individual old-time singers whom he admired: Burnett and Rutherford shine through when he performs their song *The Little Stream of Whiskey*, the Delmore Brothers are unmistakably present in his rendition of *Gonna Lay Down My Old Guitar.*

Even armed with a large repertoire and the rudiments of what was to become his own very distinctive guitar style, Doc could not play country music to country people when, as a young man in his twenties, he sought to earn a living for his wife and children.

Had he been forty or fifty years earlier, before the radio and phonograph could bring an almost unlimited variety of music and entertainment into the home of even the poorest farmer, Doc could have teamed up, as did the blind ballad singer Horton Barker, with a travelling showman. His musical talents would have drawn the people in to buy the patent medicine or to hear the pleas of a fervent evangelist, as the case might be. Even if they could not play and sing as well as Doc did, the local folk knew all those old songs anyway and their interest was focused on the latest pop tunes, on motion pictures and radio programs.

It was this time, just after the War, that Doc started to play with a few musicians in nearby Johnson City, Tennessee, a few Saturday evenings each month. They played all the old favorites from *Tea for Two* through the pop tunes of the day, mixing in country and western songs and even a bit of rhythm and blues. Doc learned the necessary new vocabulary of chords, augmented and diminished, and was soon playing those tunes all over the neck of his newly acquired electric guitar.

After seven years of playing for Saturday night dances, making the only sort of living that music ever enabled him to earn up to that point, it was not easy for Doc to grasp the situation when a couple of young men from New York City came down and asked him to lay down his electric guitar and use an acoustic instrument for their recordings. Eugene Earle, noted discographer and engineer, had joined me on my first recording trip to the home of Clarence Tom Ashley. We went to Mountain City, Tennessee, in the hope that we might interest the old banjo-picking ballad singer, whom I had met at a North Carolina fiddlers convention several months earlier, in taking up his banjo once again. Ashley, rather than play himself, had gathered around him a number of the best local musicians (q.v. Old Time Music at Clarence Ashley's, Vol. 1, Folkways, FA2355) and Doc was among them.

I asked Doc, whom I had never before met or heard, to use a non-electrified instrument and he replied that he had no other guitar and would just prefer turning the volume lower and using his own electrically amplified Gibson. A bit green as a collector, I mentioned that I did not feel that it would be suitable for the sort of recordings we had intended to make and left for the rest of the day to seek out a fine, old-time banjo player who had been with the Ashley group when I first met them.

The next day, we all piled into assorted vehicles and started off for the home of Tom Ashley's daughter. I had been riding alone on the back of a pick-up truck playing a banjo which someone had deposited there when the truck pulled off the road and Doc got out of the cab and joined me. He asked to try the banjo and taking it in his hands ripped off some of the best pure mountain picking imaginable. Those were the first few tunes I had ever heard him play and I knew immediately that a man who could pick a banjo as Doc did would understand what kind of music we were in search of some six hundred miles from New York. By the time we arrived at our destination in Saltville, Virginia, Doc and I were good friends . . . it was agreed that the electric guitar would go unused that day.

The following day was spent with Doc's wife, children and father-in-law, Gaither Carlton, in Deep Gap. Several of the recordings from this visit with the Watson family may be heard on the aforementioned Folkways recording. Doc and Gaither found it hard to believe that the cities and colleges were filled with thousands of young people who were eager to hear the very music which had more or less gone out of style in their area since the war. When I played the Folkways reissue of several early "hillbilly" recordings (Folkways Anthology of American Folk Music, FA2951-3), Gaither, a fine old-time bango picker and fiddler himself, just sat back in his chair and with a wistful expression on his face, he sighed and quietly said, "Sounds like old times."

That was in September, 1960. In March, 1961, Doc, Gaither, Tom Ashley, fiddling Fred Price, and his neighbor and buddy, Clint Howard, a strong lead singer and guitar picker, all journeyed to New York to perform at a small concert sponsored by the newly-organized Friends of Old Time Music in a downtown public school auditorium. Although Doc performed as a part of the group, doing only a few solos on the program, he was immediately singled out by the audience and each guitar break was followed by a spontaneous burst of applause. The word spread quickly and the group was soon invited to participate in a number of college folk festivals and to travel across the nation to perform at the Ash Grove in Los Angeles.

It was during the first two-week engagement at the Ash Grove that Tom Ashley, who had always been the spokesman for the group, suffered from a bad case of laryngitis and lost his voice for several days. Knowing that Doc could read Braille, I went to the local institute for the blind and purchased the necessary equipment. That night, Doc went on stage with the program card stamped out in Braille taped to the top of his guitar. He spoke on the stage much as he would with a few friends gathered about him in his house and he and the audience just sat back and enjoyed the show together.

In the years that followed, Doc performed as a soloist with increasing frequency, travelling back and forth across the country on his own. Today, his repertoire is still primarily composed of songs he knew or had heard in his early years. There were several songs which he remembered hearing but which he had never known in their entirety. These he acquired by visiting older members of the family who sing without accompaniment in the old, delicately ornamented style which was common in the area when Cecil Sharp first visited there.

Although he is best known for his remarkable style of flat-picking and his distinctive finger-picking techniques on the guitar, Doc is equally comfortable and competent singing with or without accompaniment. Those songs which he feels cannot be improved by even the most subtle support from guitar or banjo are performed in the way that he first heard music at home. It is impossible to imagine a song which he could not accompany, given time—more interesting is the choice of songs which he performs without accompaniment. Doc's exposure to music has been varied, as has his performing experience; he now emerges as one of the few artists of our time with rural roots and urban perspective who chooses to perform folk song in the traditional idiom.

Ralph Rinzler
Division of Performing Arts
Smithsonian Institution
Washington, D.C. September 1970

Introduction to
Tablature and Music Systems

READING TABLATURE

The six lines represent the six strings of the guitar, with the bass E as the bottom
line.

Arabic numbers appearing on the tablature lines indicate various fretting positions
for the left hand. For example, an "o" on the top line of the tablature staff indicates
that you play the highest sounding string unfingered by the left hand.

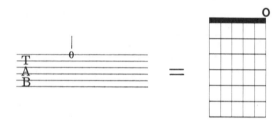

A "1" on the top line indicates that you play the highest sounding string fingered at
the 1st fret:

An entire C chord looks like this in tablature:

GUITAR SYMBOLS

S = Slide

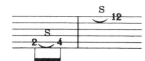

When the finger slides along a string up to a note or down to a note, this movement is indicated by a slide mark as well as the letter "s".

⌣ = Bend

A note is "bent" (or choked) when the guitar string is pushed upwards and against the finger-board by the appropriate finger of the fretting hand.

This action raises the pitch of the note approximately one-half step. Thus:

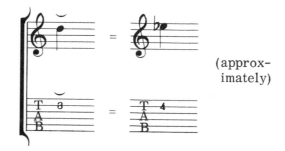

(approximately)

Strum

↓ ↑

These are the symbols for down-strum and up-strum respectively, which appear over the pertinent chords.

H = Hammer

Two notes tied together with the letter H in between indicates a "hammer-on".

A *hammered* note is not produced by plucking, or picking, but by the *hammering* action of a finger of the fretting hand:

Count: 1 & 2 3 & 4

In this example, the note "D" (open 4th string) is first plucked or picked, and the following note ("E") is sounded by *hammering* down on the 4th string/2nd fret with the middle finger of the fretting hand—while the "D" is still sounding. This action is then repeated on the 3rd string.

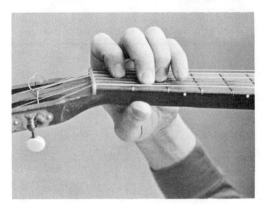

P = Pull-off

Pulling-off is the reverse of hammering.

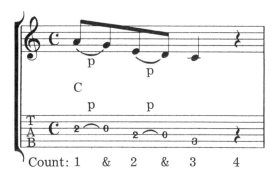

Count: 1   &   2   &   3   4

See the second beat above, the "E" is plucked, but the "D" is produced by the finger of the fretting hand *pulling-off* the 4th string/2nd fret. This action is first shown in this example on the 3rd string/first beat between notes A and G.

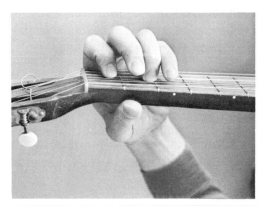

GUITAR STYLES

A collection of musical transcriptions from the playing of Doc Watson must invariably come out looking like an encyclopedia of folk guitar styles. Doc uses and has mastered them all.

Following are brief descriptions of techniques utilized in the songs in this book:

1. *Carter style:* At its simplest, this consists of alternating bass notes with chords. A basic accompaniment pattern, for example, might look like this:

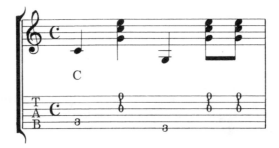

When used as a solo technique, the melody notes are picked out on the bass strings, while the chords are used as rhythmic punctuation and to fill out the total sound:

Carter style can be played using a flat-pick or, more usually, by letting the thumb pick out the bass notes while the index and middle fingers of the right hand strum or "brush" the higher-pitched strings of the chord.

2. *Flat-picking:* Doc often uses a flat-pick for fast single-string solos or for rhythmic chord strumming.

The pick should be held in a relaxed but secure manner between the thumb and index finger. The picking motion should include both up-strokes and down-strokes. Although it's hard to formulate a rule to cover every case, a down-stroke on a *downbeat* and an up-stroke on an *upbeat* will produce the smoothest results in most situations:

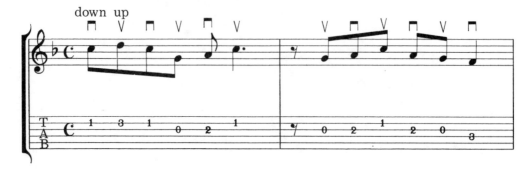

3. *Finger-picking:* Basically, in this style, the thumb keeps a steady bass rhythm (usually alternating bass notes of the chord), while the melody is picked out on the two or three higher-pitched strings by the index and middle (and occasionally ring) fingers:

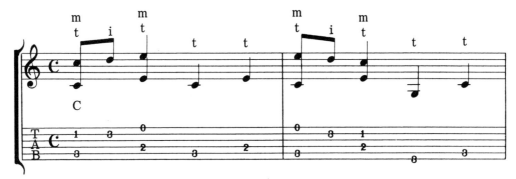

Choice of fingering is an entirely personal matter and no one way is *right*. However, throughout the book, suggestions have been made in various places, as in the example just above.

t = thumb

i = index finger

m = middle finger

a = ring finger (from the classical designation, *annular*)

DAMPING EFFECT

To get the damped (or muffled) effect, strum a chord with the thumb. (The wrist is arched.) As the thumb moves down across the strings, lower the wrist until the heel of the hand comes in contact with the sounding (vibrating) strings, thereby damping them.

OPEN TUNINGS

The standard guitar tuning (sometimes referred to as natural tuning, E tuning or Spanish tuning) is merely a convention established by usage. It should not be surprising, therefore, that imaginative musicians have come up with tunings of their own, fitted for different requirements. Several of these special tunings are used by Doc Watson and they are explained wherever they occur in the book.

USE OF THE CAPO

The capo is a mechanical device which clamps onto the fingerboard, and changes the pitch of all the open strings—the relative pitch-distance from string to string remains constant. That is, the capo shortens the *vibrating* length of each string, thereby making the pitch of each string higher.

For example, a C chord without using a capo

becomes

a Db chord when using the same fingering one fret higher with the capo on the first fret:

Doc makes extensive use of the capo as indicated throughout the book, together with the chord diagrams which are common to the new key.

CHORDS

Chord Names:

E(D)   When using a capo, the music shows two chord names for every chord;

The first is the actual pitch that you hear.

The second (in parentheses) is the chord position (i.e. chord fingering) used by Doc.

NC   Means *no chord*

Chord Symbols:

O—Open string (play without fretting)

(O)—Optional open string

(2)—Optional fretting

X—String should not be played

⌒—barre strings (i.e. press the index finger down very tightly over the strings indicated by the arc.)

BANJO SYMBOLS

Left Hand	*Right Hand*
s = slide	m = frail
h = hammer	t = pick with thumb
p = pull-off	i = pick with index
d = slide or hammer-on	

TOM DOOLEY

In the 1860's, when this story takes place, my great-grandparents were neighbors of Tom Dooley's family, and my grandparents, when they were just children, knew Tom's parents. As the story goes, Tom Dooley was not guilty of the murder of Laura Foster, although he was an accomplice in covering up the crime. Instead of the "eternal triangle" mentioned in the Kingston Trio's version, it was a quadrangle sort of thing. There were two men and two women involved in the whole affair. Mr. Grayson, the sheriff, had courted both Miss Laura Foster and Miss Annie Melton, as had Tom Dooley. Almost everyone around affirmed that Annie Melton had stuck the knife in Miss Laura's ribs and then hit her over the head. Tom Dooley, however, actually buried the girl, making himself an accomplice. Annie Melton was with Tom at Laura's burial, so she, too, was strongly suspected and was jailed. While in jail she bragged and told everyone that her neck was too pretty to put a rope around and that they'd never hang her. Of course, they never did.

Sheriff Grayson had quite a crush on Annie Melton, and he later married her. Near the end of her life Annie became very ill, and on her deathbed, she called her husband in and told him something that seemed to really crush his spirit and reason for living. What Miss Annie told her husband was what she had told the neighborhood women—that she had actually murdered Laura Foster and had let Tom Dooley go to the gallows without saying one word on his behalf. Grayson was so upset that he took his remaining family and moved completely out of this part of North Carolina and went over to the edge of Tennessee, which was just being settled.

The murder of Laura Foster happened just at the end of the Civil War, and Tom Dooley, I believe, had been a hero during the war. Dooley was the kind of guy who grows up very quickly; at the age of fourteen, he was the size of a grown man. He went into the Civil War by lying about his age and came back a hero. He was an unthinkably good old-time fiddler, and many people think that the original version, which I learned from my grandmother, has such a lilting, happy-sounding tune because the composer had tried his or her best to get into the song a little of Tom Dooley's personality as a fiddler.

TOM DOOLEY

Arranged & adapted by A.D. Watson

Medium

1. Hang your head Tom Doo-ley, Hang your head and cry; You

killed poor Lau-rie Fos-ter, And you know you're bound to die.

You left her by the roadside
Where you begged to be excused
You left her by the roadside
Then you hid her clothes and shoes.

CHORUS:
Hang your head Tom Dooley
Hang your head and cry
You killed poor Laurie Foster
And you know you're bound to die

You took her on the hillside
For to make her your wife
You took her on the hillside
And there you took her life

You dug the grave four feet long
And you dug it three feet deep
You rolled the cold clay over her
And tromped it with your feet.

Chorus

"Trouble, oh it's trouble
A-rollin through my breast
As long as I'm a-livin' boys
They ain't a-gonna let me rest

I know they're gonna hang me
Tomorrow I'll be dead
Though I never even harmed a hair
On poor little Laurie's head."

Chorus

In this world and one more
Then reckon where I'll be
If it wasn't for Sheriff Grayson
I'd be in Tennessee.

"You can take down my old violin
And play it all you please.
For at this time tomorrow, boys
It'll be of no use to me.

Chorus

At this time tomorrow
Where do you reckon I'll be
Away down yonder in the holler
Hangin on a white oak tree.

Chorus

TOM DOOLEY – Basic Accompaniment Pattern

Capo 2nd Fret/Carter Style: the thumb picks the bass note while the index and middle fingers "brush" the top strings of the chord up and down.

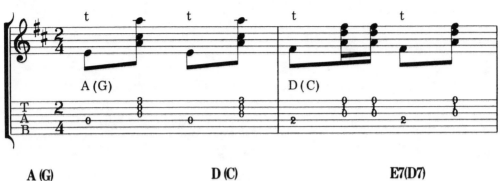

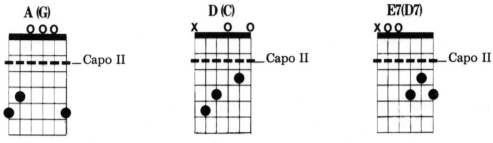

TOM DOOLEY – Guitar Break

DOC'S GUITAR

This was my inspiration from a tune that I had heard Merle Travis do. Travis picked a tune called *Blue Smoke*, and he played the "thing" out of a D minor barred chord. He didn't use the cheater or capo—I always call it the cheater—to play the thing. I got the idea for *Doc's Guitar* from the little roll that Travis used, and I added a few notions of my own. Sometimes when I pick the tune, I think of a bunch of kittens running, because it sounds sort of playful. It's not really hard, it's just fast.

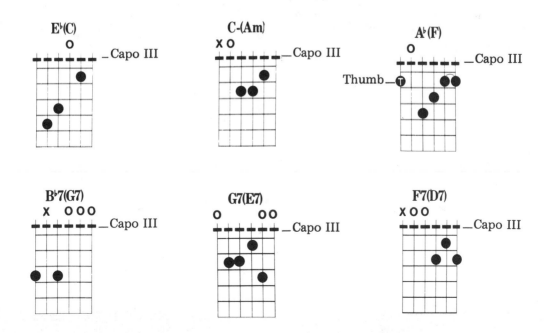

DOC'S GUITAR

By A.D. Watson

Finger-Pick/Capo 3rd Fret

BLACK MOUNTAIN RAG

This tune was inspired by three or four different fiddlers. First, the fellow who originated the tune, as far as I'm concerned, is an old boy, Leslie Keith. I heard him play *Black Mountain Rag* or *Black Mountain Blues*—he would call it by either name—and I picked around with it a little on the guitar. Then, I began to hear other fiddlers like Tommy Jackson and Curly Fox play it: my arrangement on the guitar is closer to theirs than it is to the original because some of the things Leslie Keith did in the old-time fiddle style, I just couldn't find on my guitar. I don't know how he gets it all in there.

Black Mountain Rag was the first fiddle tune, as such, that I tried doing on the guitar. Incidentally, I tried fiddling for two or three years when I was in my teens. I could note the left hand all right, but when it came down to that bowing hand, I must have sounded like a rusty door hinge.

BLACK MOUNTAIN RAG

Flat-Pick/Capo 3rd Fret

Arranged & adapted by A.D. Watson

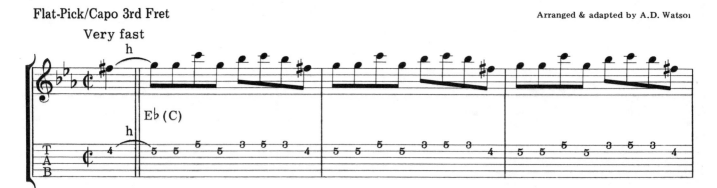

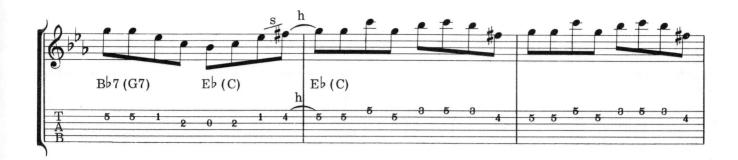

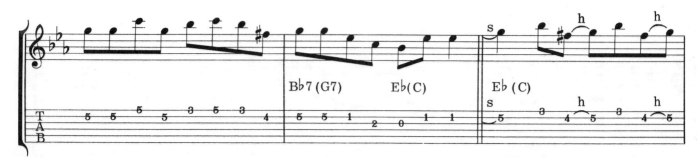

THE TRAIN THAT CARRIED MY GIRL FROM TOWN

Ever since I can remember hearing music on our family's graphophone, I've heard this tune. Frank Hutchinson is the guy who did the record of *The Train That Carried My Girl From Town*; he tuned the guitar to an open D and played it with a bottle neck or a pocket knife. But I decided that if you get a thumb pick or two in your pocket, you are toting enough junk around, so I just fret the thing in an open tuning with my finger and occasionally throw in a bar or two.

The Train That Carried My Girl From Town can be done in any number of ways. My son, Merle, and I are thinking of recording a bluegrass version at a faster clip. On the twelve-string it's also fun; it really gives the song a lot of drive and gives you a feeling of a big old locomotive going down the track—the way they used to sound.

THE TRAIN THAT CARRIED MY GIRL FROM TOWN

Arranged & adapted by A.D. Watson

Moderately fast

1. There goes The Train That Car-ried My Girl From Town,__ If I knowed her num - ber Lord, I'd flag __ her down. __ Wish to the Lord that the train would wreck__ kill the en - gi - neer ____ and break the fire - man's neck. Hey, that Train__ That Carried My Girl From Town. Hey __ yeah __ hey __ yeah.

Basic Accompaniment Pattern

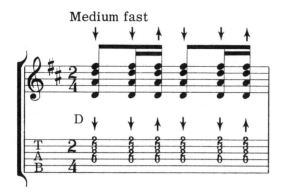

Where was you when the train left town?
I was standing on the corner with my head hung down,
If I had a gun I'd let the hammer down,
Lord, I'd shoot that rounder took my girl from town.
Hey, that train, etc.

Rations on the table and my coffee's getting cold,
And some dirty rounder took my jelly roll,
Hello Central, give me six-o-nine,
I want to talk to that woman of mine.
Hey, that train, etc.

Ashes to ashes and dust to dust,
Can you show me the woman that a man can trust,
There goes my girl, somebody bring her back,
Cause she's got her hand in my money sack.
Hey, that train, etc.

THE TRAIN THAT CARRIED MY GIRL FROM TOWN – Guitar Break

Flat-Pick

Fast (Train whistle effect)

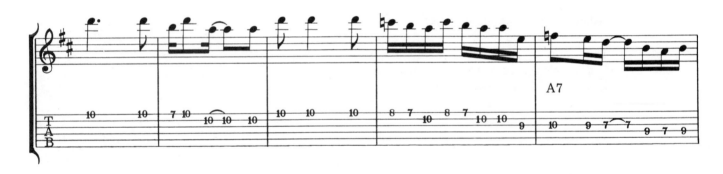

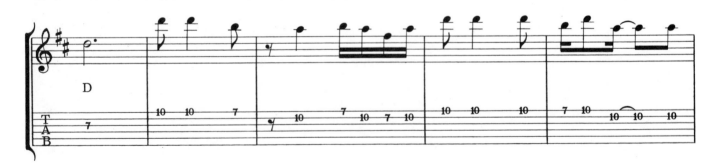

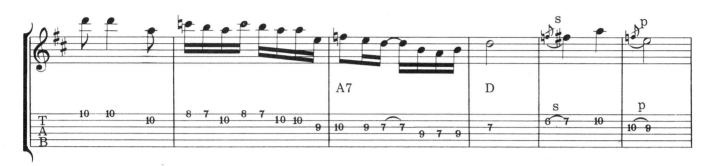

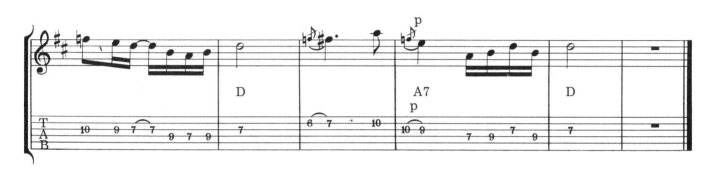

DEEP RIVER BLUES

This blues was introduced to me in the late thirties by a Delmore Brothers recording. When I first began to hear the tune, I was fascinated by the sounds they got out of the little tenor guitar—the four-string—and the regular flattop box. I never could figure a way to get even a resemblance of the sound that they got until I began to hear Merle Travis pick the guitar. When Merle plays the guitar, he gets a rhythmic beat going by bouncing his thumb back and forth on the bass strings, which he mutes with the edge of the palm of his hand. I worked out that little back-up part first, but it took me about ten years before I got the whole thing sounding the way I wanted it.

DEEP RIVER BLUES

Arranged & adapted by A.D. Watson

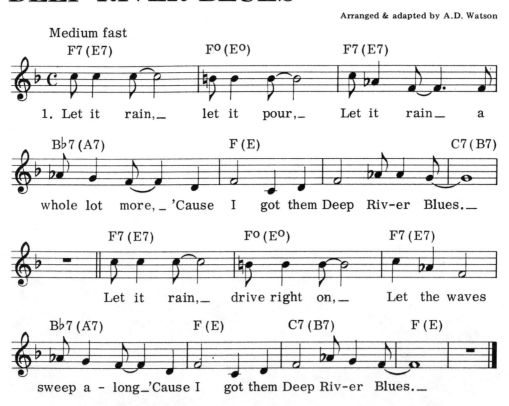

My old gal's a good old pal
And she looks like a water fowl
When I get them Deep River Blues

They ain't no one to cry for me
And the fish all go out on a spree
When I get them Deep River Blues

Give me back my old boat
I'm gonna sail if she'll float
Cause I got them Deep River Blues

I'm goin' back to Muscle Shoals
Times are better there I'm told
Cause I got them Deep River Blues

If my boat sinks with me
I'll go down don't you see
Cause I got them Deep River Blues

Now I'm gonna say goodbye
And if I sink just let me die
Cause I got them Deep River Blues

Repeat First Verse

Basic Accompaniment Pattern

Finger-Pick/Capo 1st Fret

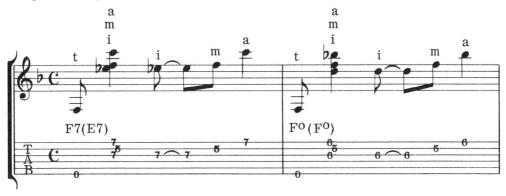

F7(E7) F°(F°)

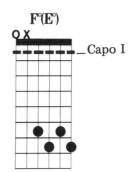

F7(E7)

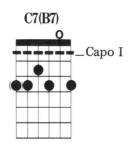

F°(E°)

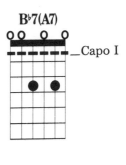

B♭7(A7)

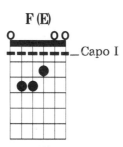

F (E)

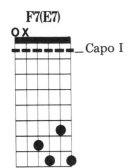

C7(B7)

DEEP RIVER BLUES – Guitar Break

THE CALL OF THE ROAD

The Call Of The Road is a thing I put together in the early fifties. A very dear friend of mine was being led away from his home and family by some of the things that don't mean anything once you've thoroughly examined them, you know, just big kicks. That's where this song came from—my thoughts about my good friend. Incidentally, he got back on the right track and straightened out. I don't think this song had anything to do with it, because he had the right stuff in him to begin with.

Basic Accompaniment Pattern

Flat-Pick

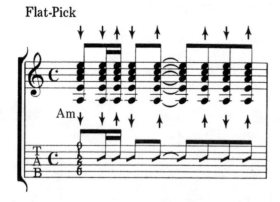

THE CALL OF THE ROAD

Moderately

Words and music by Arthel "Doc" Watson

1. When I was a boy I had to know__
What I would find just o - ver the hill.
And while still a lad I had to__ go
And so you see I'm ram - bl - in' still.__

Life's golden cup was filled for me,
With happiness in measures untold;
But I left the one who cared for me,
A treasure worth so much more than
  gold.

Young men that roam take heed to
  this,
The call of the road can be so unkind;
It will lead you on like a fickle kiss,
And a wasted life is all you'll ever
  find.

THE CALL OF THE ROAD - Guitar Break

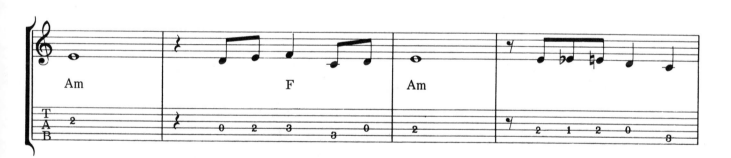

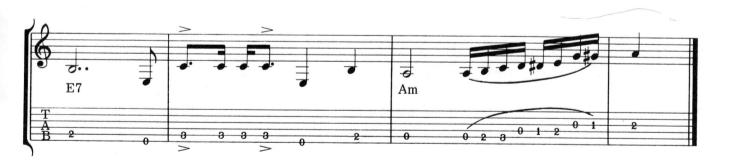

OMIE WISE

This ballad was written about a tragedy which took place in the spring or summer of 1808. Naomi Wise, a little orphan girl, was being brought up by Squire Adams, a gent who had a pretty good name in the community as a morally decent human being. Omie, however, was seeing a ne'er-do-well named John Lewis, who never meant anything about anything serious, except some of his meanness. John Lewis courted the girl, seemingly until she became pregnant, and he decided that he'd get rid of her in a secret sort of way. He persuaded her to skip off with him and get married, then pushed her into the water and drowned her. Everyone knew that he had been mean to Omie, and when the body was taken out of the water, there was evidence that she had been beaten quite a lot.

I learned the song from my mother and some verses from my father-in-law, Gaither Carlton. Later, a distant cousin of mine who lives nearby, Dolly Greer, put the final touches on it by helping me with some verses that I had forgotten.

OMIE WISE

Arranged & adapted by A.D. Watson

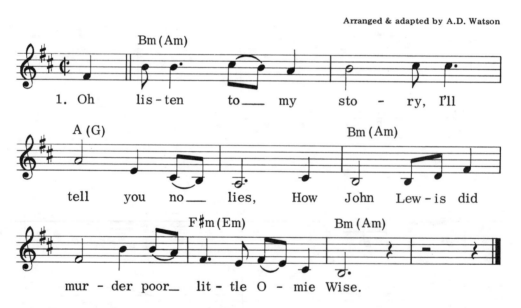

1. Oh lis-ten to my sto-ry, I'll tell you no lies, How John Lew-is did mur-der poor lit-tle O-mie Wise.

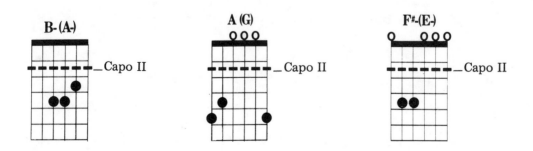

Basic Accompaniment Pattern

Finger-Pick/Capo 2nd Fret

Moderately fast

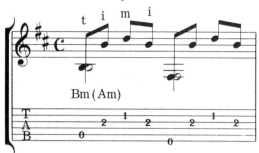

Bm (Am)

He told her to meet him at Adams's Springs.
He promised her money and other fine things.

So, fool-like she met him at Adams's Springs.
No money he brought her nor other fine things.

"Go with me, little Omie, and away we will go.
"We'll go and get married and no one will know."

She climbed up behind him and away they did go,
But off to the river where deep waters flow.

"John Lewis, John Lewis, will you tell me your mind?
"Do you intend to marry me or leave me behind?"

"Little Omie, little Omie, I'll tell you my mind.
"My mind is to drown you and leave you behind."

"Have mercy on my baby and spare me my life,
"I'll go home as a beggar and never be your wife."

He kissed her and hugged her and turned her around,
Then pushed her in deep waters where he knew that she would drown.

He got on his pony and away he did ride,
As the screams of little Omie went down by his side.

T'was on a Thursday morning, the rain was pouring down,
When the people searched for Omie but she could not be found.

Two boys went a-fishin' one fine summer day,
And saw little Omie's body go floating away.

They threw their net around her and drew her to the bank.
Her clothes all wet and muddy, they laid her on a plank.

Then sent for John Lewis to come to that place—
And brought her out before him so that he might see her face.

He made no confession but they carried him to jail,
No friends nor relations would go on his bail.

OMIE WISE – Guitar Break

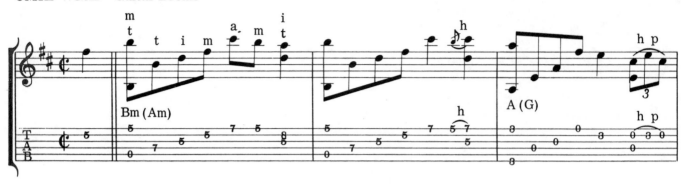

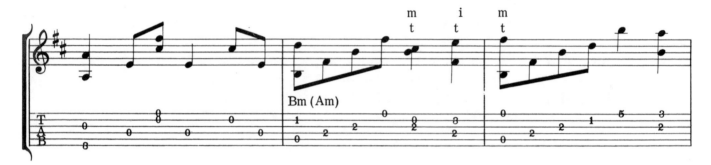

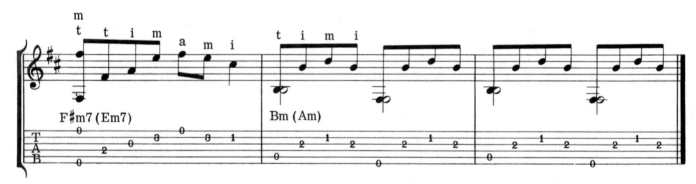

MATTY GROVES

I learned the words of *Matty Groves* from Dolly Greer, except for a few lines, which I doctored a little bit to make them rhyme. The melody was taught to me by Stewart Yonce of Lenoire, North Carolina. I really love both the music and the words of *Matty Groves*; the music itself always gets to me, and the words appeal to me as a story of high adventure.

Basic Accompaniment Pattern

Finger-Pick

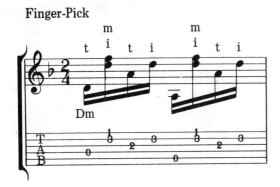

MATTY GROVES

New music by Stewart Yonce
Additional words and arrangement by
Dolly Greer and Arthel "Doc" Watson

Moderately

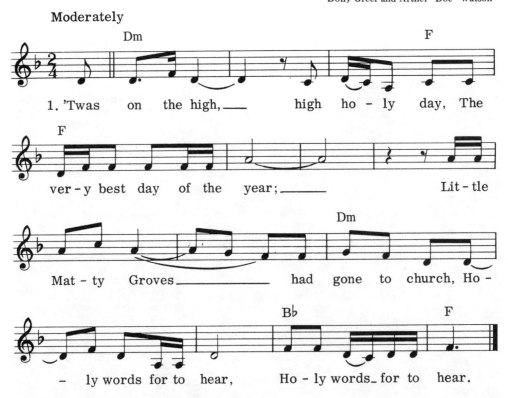

1. 'Twas on the high,— high ho - ly day, The ver - y best day of the year; ___ Lit - tle Mat - ty Groves___ had gone to church, Ho - ly words for to hear, Ho - ly words_ for to hear.

The first to come down was dressed in red,
And the second one dressed in green,
The third to come down was Lord Daniel's wife,
As fair as any queen,
Just as fair as any queen.

Then Matty Groves says to one of his men,
"See the fair one dressed in white,
"Although she is Lord Daniel's wife,
"I'll be with her tonight,
"I'll be with her tonight."

The little foot page was a-standin' by,
And he heard every word that was said,
He says that Lord Daniel shall know tonight,
Before I go to bed,
Before I go to bed.

He had fifteen miles for to go that night,
And ten of them he run,
He run till he come to the broke down bridge,
Then he bent to his breast and he swum,
He bent to his breast and he swum.

He swum till he come to where the grass was green,
He took to his feet and he run,
He run till he come to Lord Daniel's gate,
He rattled at the bells and they rung,
Yes, he rattled at the bells and they rung.

"What news, what news," Lord Daniel says,
"What news to me have you brung?"
"Little Matty Groves is in the bed with your wife,
"And their hearts both beat as one,
"And their hearts both beat as one."

"Now if the truth you've told to me,
"A rich man you shall be;
"But if a lie you've told to me,
"I'll hang you to a tree,
"I'll hang you to a tree."

He gathered him up about fifty good men,
And he done it with a free good will;
Then he popped his bugle unto his lips,
And he blowed it loud and shrill,
He blowed it loud and shrill.

"I'd better get up," said little Matty Groves,
"I'd better get up and go;
"I know your husband is a-comin' home,
"For I heard his bugle blow,
"I heard his bugle blow."

"Lay down, lay down, my precious one,
"Lay down and go to sleep;
"It's only my father's shepherd's horn,
"And he's a-callin' for his sheep,
"He's a-callin' for his sheep."

So they lay down together again,
And they soon were fast asleep;
And when they awoke it was broad daylight,
Lord Daniel at their feet,
Lord Daniel at their feet.

"Get up from there you naked man,
"And put you on some clothes;
"I never intend for to have it said,
"That a naked man I slo',
"That a naked man I slo'."

"Oh give me a chance," said little Matty Groves,
"A chance to fight for my life;
"For there you have two very fine swords,
"And me not as much as a knife,
"And me not as much as a knife."

"Oh yes, I have two very fine swords,
"And they cost me deep in the purse;
"You may have the finest one
"And I will take the worst,
"Yes I will take the worst."

Then Matty Groves struck the very first lick,
And he wounded Lord Daniel sore;
Lord Daniel struck the very next lick,
And he drove Matty Groves to the floor,
He drove Matty Groves to the floor.

Then he taken his lady by the hand,
And he set her on his knee;
And he says, "Now which do you love the best,
"Little Matty Groves or me,
"Little Matty Groves or me?"

"Very well, I like your rosy cheeks,
"Very well, I like your chin;
"But better I love little Matty Groves,
"Than you and all your kin,
"Than you and all your kin."

"You can dig my grave on a pretty green hill,
"Dig it wide and deep;
"And put little Matty Groves in my arms,
"Lord Daniel at my feet,
"Lord Daniel at my feet."

THE OLD MAN BELOW

In this song you can picture an old man whose wife has just died, leaving him five or six daughters, and the oldest of them is old enough, maybe, to bake a little hoecake in the ashes or cook a piece of meat. Well, the old man is a natural-born woodsman, and he does enough hunting and farming to keep them all alive. He loves the girls, but he just doesn't know how to manage so many of them. Because he doesn't know exactly what to do with all of his daughters, he's willing to marry them off as soon as he can, as long as it's to somebody with a little nerve and somebody who he thinks might work for the young lady and treat her right. The way the song goes, the old man comes in and finds a young boy there with his daughters, who he's usually pretty strict with. When the boy braves right up to the girls' father, the old man likes his nerve and says, "Pull you up a chair, boy, and sit down and rest." It's just a courting song with a little fun and humor added.

I had never heard the song until a short time before we did the *Home Again* album. Ralph Rinzler came down here one summer and was over at Gaither Carlton's house. Gaither just doesn't like to sing at all, but somehow (I half thought Ralph might have slipped him a little taste of some good booze, but in fact, that didn't happen) he sang a lot of songs from his boyhood, and *The Old Man Below* is one of those.

Basic Accompaniment Pattern

Play Carter Style: the thumb picks the bass notes while the index and middle fingers "brush" the top strings of the chord up and down.

THE OLD MAN BELOW

Words and Music by
Gaither W. Carlton and Arthel "Doc" Watson

Moderately fast

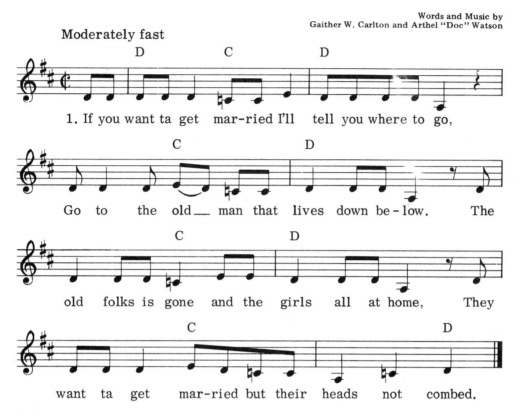

1. If you want ta get mar-ried I'll tell you where to go,
Go to the old — man that lives down be - low. The
old folks is gone and the girls all at home, They
want ta get mar-ried but their heads not combed.

Children, children a-cryin' for bread,
Go and build on a fire just as high as your head;
Then you rake in the ashes for to lie in the dough,
And the name that you give them is dough boy dough.

They call me into supper and I thought I'd go eat,
I went to the table for to carve on the meat;
Had an old dull knife and I had not a fork,
I sawed about an hour and I never made a mark.

I sawed another hour and I got him in my plate,
Then the girls said, "Young man, you'd better wait.
"Young man, young man, you better run,
"For the old man's a-comin' with his double barreled gun."

The old man a-grinnin' as he came a-walkin' in,
Patches on his britches and whiskers on his chin;
He had an old hat that he wore the year around,
But he had neither hat nor the brim, nor the crown.

I stood right there just as brave as a bear,
And I wiggled my finger in the old man's hair;
Then he says, "My man, I think you're the best,
"Pull you up a chair, son, and set down and rest."

Repeat First Verse

SOUTHBOUND

A few years back, we were working in New York for a few weeks. I think we had done a couple of recording sessions, and maybe a couple of weeks at the Gaslight. Anyway, Merle, from the first time he had been to New York City, had decided he didn't like the place. There was just too much noise and not enough fresh air, and you know how that appeals to a country boy. He got to sitting around there doodling with the guitar, like with a pencil on a piece of paper, and all at once he began to come up with some pretty good-sounding things. He didn't come up with words right away, but just thought a lot about them. He'd go out and walk the streets because he was so lonesome, and he actually blistered his heels just loafing during the day. *Southbound* is a good example of a homesick country boy in a big city somewhere, wanting to go home; he just wanted to get out of there.

Basic Accompaniment Pattern

Flat-Pick/
"Damp" the strum on all off-beat attacks.

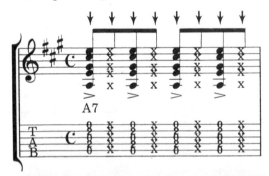

SOUTHBOUND

Words and music by Merle Watson and Arthel "Doc" Watson

Moderately bright

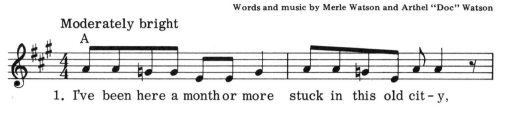

1. I've been here a month or more stuck in this old cit-y,

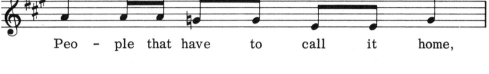

Peo - ple that have to call it home,

they're the ones I pit - y, Lord, I'm home - sick,

blues are the on - ly songs I ev - er seem to pick,

I get out and walk the street till

I get blis-ters on my feet, I'm South Bound. ___

I'm all right till late at night I'm sittin' by my window,
I count sheep but I can't sleep for listening to that train blow,
I begin to pine when I hear that great big engine rollin' down the line.
I'm a-goin' back and spend some time where I can have fun when I ain't got a dime,
I'm southbound.

Southbound she's a-burnin' the ground and I don't mean maybe,
Sure am glad I caught this train, I wanna see my baby,
Lord, I'm lonesome, long to see those hills that I came from.
Listen to that engine rattle and roar, takin' me back home once more,
I'm southbound.

SOUTHBOUND – Guitar Break

A ROVIN' ON A WINTER'S NIGHT

To me, *A-Rovin' On A Winter's Night* is just about one of the prettiest old-time love songs that you could hope to find anywhere. I'll never forget the night when Ralph Rinzler and I went down to Dolly and Len Greer's house. Outside you could hear the sound of those little frogs that you hear in the spring around the edge of a stream or a swampy area, and in the distance you could hear an occasional whip-poorwill. It was in this setting that Dolly sang *A-Rovin' On A Winter's Night*. I had never heard it before and I thought it was so beautiful.

You can picture an old boy who has an indescribable love for a girl. He knows that he has to go on a long journey, but doesn't give his reasons. He knows, just as well as he knows that his heart's thumping in his chest from his excitement at looking at the girl, that she's not going to be his when he returns. He's going to try and drown that sorrow by getting out and roaming around with some of his buddies and soaking up a little good vintage wine—kind of warm his heart and cool off that dread of losing that pretty girl.

Basic Accompaniment Pattern

Finger-Pick

A-ROVIN' ON A WINTER'S NIGHT

Additional words and music by
Dolly Greer and Arthel "Doc" Watson

Moderately

1. A - rov - in' On A Win - ter's Night, And a-drink - in' good old wine; Think-in' a - bout that pret-ty lit - tle girl, That broke this heart of mine.

She is just like a butter rose
That blooms in the month of June.
Or like some musical instrument
That's just been lately tuned.

Perhaps it's a trip to a foreign land
A trip to France or Spain.
But if I should go ten thousand miles
I'm a-comin' back again.

And it's who's a-gonna shoe your poor
little feet
Who's a-gonna glove your little hands.
Who's a-gonna kiss your sweet little
lips
Honey, who's a-gonna be your man?

I'll love you till the sea runs dry
And the rocks all melt in the sun.
I'll love you till the day I die
Though you will never be my own.

Repeat First Verse

A-ROVIN' ON A WINTER'S NIGHT – Guitar Break

GEORGIE

I learned the words to *Georgie*, except for two or three lines, from Cecil Sharp's edition, and the melody from my father-in-law, Gaither Carlton. Gaither did a beautiful job of it on the fiddle, but he never could quite get the sound that suited us in the right key where I could sing it comfortably. I once thought of having him play it with me on a recording, but for that reason I couldn't. He was comfortable in a certain key. You know how ethnic musicians are—I'm pretty bad for that myself.

Georgie is an American version of the old Scottish ballad called *Geordie*, and was evidently written after a true happening, as most of the old ballads were. The boy thinks that if he's honest in the king's court of law and tells the whole truth, he will not be accused of stealing the king's horses and will not be sent to the gallows. But, bless his heart, by defending himself at the bar, he does get hung.

Basic Accompaniment Pattern

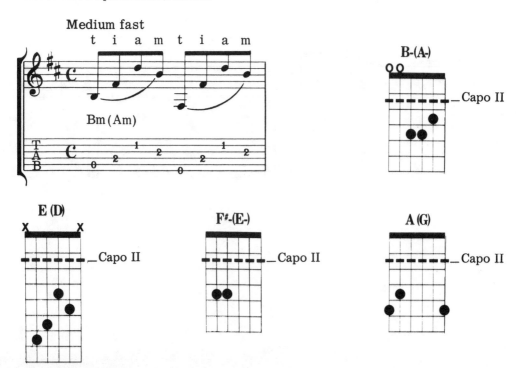

54

GEORGIE

Adaptation and additional words and music
by Gaither Carlton and Arthel "Doc" Watson

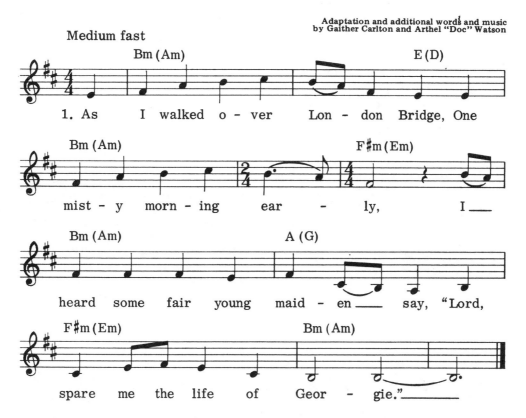

Medium fast

Bm (Am)   E (D)

1. As I walked o - ver Lon - don Bridge, One

Bm (Am)   F♯m (Em)

mist - y morn - ing ear - ly, I

Bm (Am)   A (G)

heard some fair young maid - en ___ say, "Lord,

F♯m (Em)   Bm (Am)

spare me the life of Geor - gie." ___

"Go saddle me up my milk white steed,
"And bridle him so gaily.
"Then I'll ride away to the kings' high court,
"And plead for the life of Georgie.

She rode all day and she rode all night,
Till she was wet and weary.
Then combing back her long yellow hair,
She plead for the life of Georgie.

She pulled out a purse all filled with gold,
Just like you've never seen many.
And she said, "Young lawyers fee yourselves,
"And plead for the life of Georgie."

But Georgie rode up and he plead for himself.
He says, "I never murdered any.
"But I stole sixteen of the king's best steeds
"And sold them in Romany."

Then the oldest lawyer at the bar
Says, "George, I'm sorry for you.
"But your own confession condemns
"May the Lord have mercy upon you."
you to die,

As Georgie was a-walkin' through the streets
He bid farewell to many
Then he bid farewell to his own true love
Which grieved him worst than any.

If I was over on yonder hill
Where kisses I've had a-plenty.
With my sword and my pistol by my side
I'd fight for the life of Georgie.

Georgie was hanged with a golden cord,
Just like you've never seen many.
For he was a member of the royal race,
And loved by a virtuous lady.

GEORGIE – Guitar Break

F. F. V.

This is another song that I learned from my mother. I've been told that this version is the closest to the original which can be found. I learned that the man who wrote *F. F. V.* was very likely a Negro who worked for the railroad as an engine wiper; supposedly, he put himself in the position of Jack Dixon, the fireman, when he wrote the song. The train wreck of his song actually did happen, just out of the C & O Tunnel, but no one knows whether Jack really did jump. Also, it is known that George's mother was not still alive at the time of the wreck; a few changes and additions were made on the actual event to make the story a little more sentimental and pretty.

E (C)
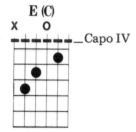

A7(F7)
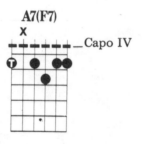

F#7(D7)
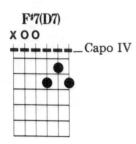

B7(G7)
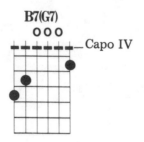

Basic Accompaniment Pattern

Flat-Pick/Capo 4th Fret

E (C)

F. F. V.

By Arthel "Doc" Watson and Mrs. G.D. Watson

Moderately

E (C)

1. Oh yon - der comes old F. F. V., the

A7 (F7)   E (C)

fast - est on — the line, Run - nin' on — the

F#7 (D7)   B7 (G7)

C. and O. just twen-ty min-utes be - hind time.

E (C)

She's roll - in' on the C. and O.— where the

A7 (F7)   E (C)

quar - ters on— the line, A - wait - in' her strict

B7 (G7)   E (C)

or - ders from the sta - tion just be - hind._____

Now when she got to Hampton, an engineer was there,
His name was Georgie Allo, oh with his curly hair.
His fireman was Jack Dixon, a-standin' by his side,
A-waitin' their strict orders when in the cab to ride.

Then Georgie's mother came to him with a bucket on her arm,
Sayin', "Georgie son, be careful, be careful how you run.
"There's many a man that's lost his life tryin' to make lost time,
"But if you run your engine right, you'll get there just on time."

"Mother, oh dear mother, your advice I'll take heed,
"But I know my engine is all right and I'm sure that she will speed.
"Goin' up this road I mean to go at the speed of a cannon ball,
"And when I blow for the stockyard gap, gonna make them hear my call."

Then he said to his fireman, Jack, "I want a little more extra speed,
"I'm gonna run old Number Four the fastest she's ever been seen.
"Goin' up this road I mean to go at a speed unknown to all,
"And when I blow for the Big Bend Tunnel I'll make them hear my call."

Then he said to his fireman, Jack, "A rock ahead I see,
"And I know that death is a-waitin' to grasp both you and me.
"It's from this engine you must leap, your darlin' life to save,
"I want you to be an engineer when I'm sleepin' in my grave."

George would not leave his engine so destined to be his fate,
And he told his fireman, "You must jump before it is too late!"
Jack Dixon from that engine leaped to the river that was foamin' high,
And he waved goodbye to Georgie as old Number Four flew by.

Goin' up the road she darted and against the rock she crashed,
The engine then turned upside down, poor Georgie's breast did smash.
His head went against the firebox door and the flames were rollin' high,
He had said he was born an engineer on the C & O to die.

Georgie's mother came to him sayin', "Son, what have you done?"
"Too late, too late, dear mother, my race on earth is run.
"But if I had a local freight, the truth to you I'll tell,
"I'd take her to grip and before no time I'd drop her into hell."

The doctor told poor Georgie, your life cannot be saved
Murdered on this railroad line to be laid in a lonesome grave,
His face was covered up with blood and his eyes you could not see,
The last words poor Georgie said was, "Nearer My God To Thee".

F. F. V. – Guitar Break

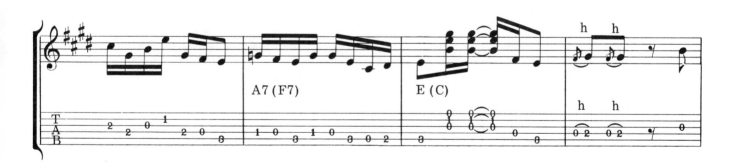

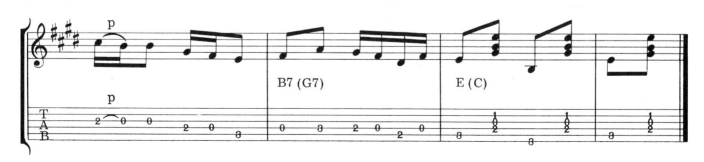

LOVIN' EMMA

I don't know anything about *Lovin' Emma* except that it's a courting song about a fellow who has a very passionate feeling for a young lady, and he wants her for his own. I learned it from my father-in-law, Gaither Carlton.

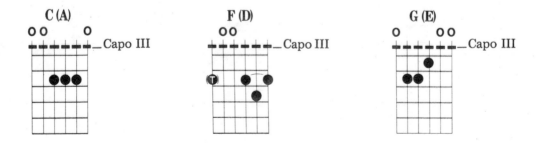

Basic Accompaniment Pattern

Finger-Pick/Capo 3rd Fret

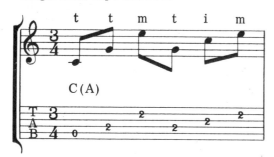

LOVIN' EMMA

Words and music by
Gaither W. Carlton and Arthel "Doc" Watson

Your cheeks are like ro - ses your sweet voice so

fine. God bless you sweet Em - ma, I

wish you were mine. Your breath smells so

sweet _____ Like the dew on the vine God

bless you Lov-in' Em-ma, I wish you were mine. _____

I'll build us a cabin
On a mountain so fine
So I can sit by you
And tell you my mind

Chorus

My mind is to marry
And never to part
The first time I saw you
You wounded my heart

Chorus

LOVIN' EMMA - Guitar Break

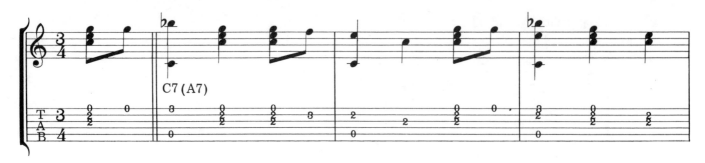

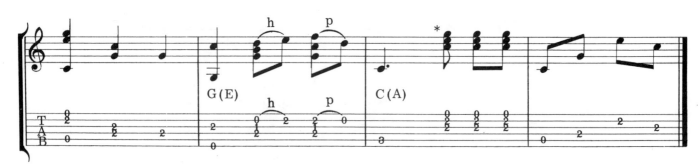

*Brushed with index and middle fingers as in Carter Style.

SHADY GROVE

I learned *Shady Grove* from my dad. I may have learned a couple of verses from Clarence Ashley, but my dad is mainly responsible for teaching me the song.

Shady Grove, to me, means my wife, Rosa Lee and my memories of going to see her when I was a boy. She was a sweet country girl, and very often I might go to her house unexpectedly, and she might be barefooted, you know. To me, she was the best thing God ever created, there wasn't any use in talking about it. That's what *Shady Grove* means to me—happiness. It also expresses memories of my dad and things that I can't remember, but can almost remember, as when something is mentioned and you can look back farther than your own lifetime and your own memory. Somehow you are almost there, amongst the log rollings, the corn shuckings, and the happy times that people had when there wasn't so much hustle and bustle all over the country. People had time to enjoy themselves and think about each other as friends and neighbors. Those are the things that *Shady Grove* mean to me.

SHADY GROVE

Arranged and adapted by A. Doc Watson

Shad - y Grove my lit-tle love Shad - y Grove I say,

Shad - y Grove my lit-tle love I'm bound to go a - way.

Cheeks as red as a blooming rose
And eyes are the prettiest brown,
She's the darling of my heart
Sweetest girl in town.
Shady Grove, my etc.

I wish I had a big fine horse
And corn to feed him on,
And Shady Grove to stay at home,
And feed him while I'm gone.
Shady Grove, my etc.

Went to see my Shady Grove
She was standing in the door,
Her shoes and stockin's in her hand
And her little bare feet on the floor.
Shady Grove, my etc.

When I was a little boy
I wanted a barlow knife,
And now I want little Shady Grove
To say she'll be my wife.
Shady Grove, my etc.

A kiss from pretty little Shady Grove
Is sweet as brandy wine,
And there ain't no girl in this old
    world
That's prettier than mine.
Shady Grove, my etc.

Basic Accompaniment Pattern

Flat-Pick/Capo 1st Fret

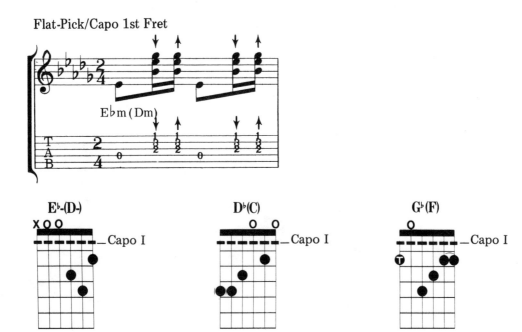

SHADY GROVE – Guitar Break

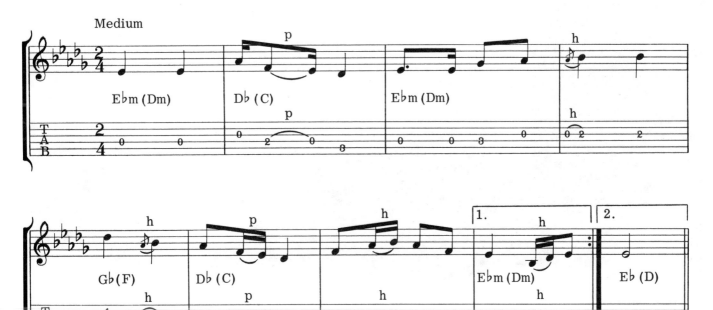

SPIKE DRIVER'S BLUES

This arrangement of *Spike Driver's Blues* is just a crude imitation of John Hurt; it's not even a reasonable facsimile. It is one of my most beloved tunes. The first time I heard that record, I must have been about eight years old. In one sense it's a very sorrowful blues; the guy is homesick and getting awfully tired of the railroad crew. In another sense, there is that happy sound of John Hurt in there. I don't care what kind of blues he played, it was always happy in a way.

SPIKE DRIVER'S BLUES

Finger-Pick/Capo 2nd Fret

by John Hurt

John_ Hen-ry was a steel driv - in' boy

but he went down, Yes, he_ went

down, He_went down. John_

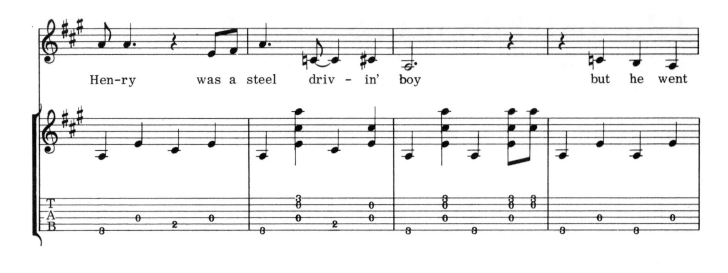

Hen-ry   was a steel   driv – in' boy   but he went

down.

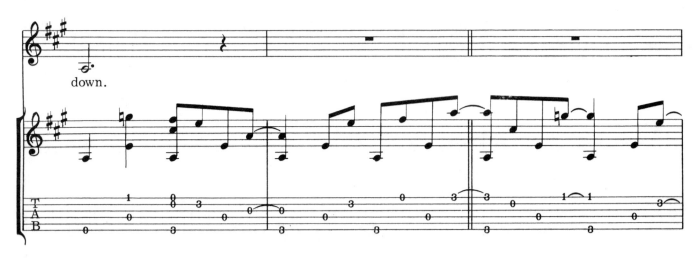

Guitar Break

Got them mean old spike driver blues
And they won't go
They won't go
No, they won't go
Got them mean old spike driver blues
And they won't go.

John Henry he left his hammer
Laid the side the road
Laid the side the road
Laid the side the road
John Henry he left his hammer
Laid the side the road.

It's a long way from East Colorado
Honey, to my home
Honey, to my home
Honey, to my home
It's a long way from East Colorado
Honey, to my home.

Take this hammer and carry to the
    Capt'n
And tell'm I'm gone
Tell'm I'm gone
You tell'm I'm gone
Take this hammer and carry to the
    Capt'n
And tell'm I'm gone
You're sure he's gone.

NOTHING TO IT

Nothing To It is, in reality, *I Don't Love Nobody*, by Riley Puckett and Gid Tanner; Gid Tanner or Clayton McMichen does the fiddling on the old recording, and Riley Puckett sings the verses. In one of the verses he sings, "I don't love nobody,/ nobody don't love me./ The girls all want my money,/ they don't want me./ I just want to be happy,/ I just want to be free./ I don't love nobody,/ nobody don't love me."

When John Pilla and I did it on the record, we played it just about as fast as we could and still get the notes in. When we finished, Dave Gude, who worked for Vanguard then, asked me what I called it. I said, "Aw, *Nothing To It*, I reckon, since I didn't do it so well." I forgot to go back and tell him that the tune's real name was *I Don't Love Nobody*, so it just went down on the record as *Nothing To It*.

NOTHING TO IT

Traditional dance tune—arranged by Arthel "Doc" Watson

Flat-Pick

Very fast

74

THE INTOXICATED RAT

This arrangement of *The Intoxicated Rat* is something I thought up from the Dixon Brothers' original version of the song. There was an old fellow who came in drunk one night—I mean he was really intoxicated—and fell down and spilled a bottle of whiskey. Evidently, a rat in that little shack where the old man lived came out, drank up some of the booze, and got quite intoxicated. Dorsey Dixon's father told him the story—I don't know how much of it is true—and he and his brother Howard decided they'd do a song about the little rat.

I added the sound effects of the cork popping and the whiskey running out of the bottle because I thought children would really enjoy them. I thought up my arrangement a couple of months before I did the recording session, and I had to do it on stage a few times just to make sure I had the nerve to try it on a record.

Basic Accompaniment Pattern

Either flat-pick or thumb-pick the bass notes while the index, middle and ring fingers pluck the top three notes of the chord.

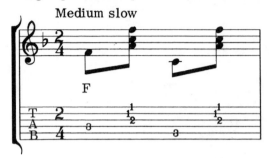

THE INTOXICATED RAT

by Dorsey Dixon & Wade Mainer

Verse:

3. There's a lit-tle old rat in his hid-in' place__ He got that whis-key scent He slipped right up 'n' he got him a ssshp 'n' back to his hole he went. Says

Chorus:

back to his hole he went Back to his hole he went He slipped right up 'n' he got him a ssshp

(He's drinkin' it all) 'n' back to his hole he went.

First two verses half-spoken, half-sung to the melody of verse 3 below

The other night when I come in
So drunk I couldn't see,
I hooked my toe in the old doormat
And fell as flat as I could be.

I had me a little old bottle 'a' booze
(And I didn't have n'more),
When I fell down—the cork flew outta the bottle,
(Pop!) (Glug glug glug glug, etc.)
'N' spilled it.

He slipped right up to my puddle 'a' gin
And he lapped up more and more,
He says, "Doggone my red-eyed soul
"I'm a-gonna get drunk once more."

CHORUS:
"I'm a-gonna get drunk once more
"I'm a-gonna get drunk once more."
He says, "Doggone my red-eyed soul,
"I'm a-gonna get drunk once more."

He washed his face with his front paws
And on his hind legs he sat,
And he's a gettin' pretty high when he winked one eye
And he says, "Hey where's that old tom-cat?"

CHORUS:
"Now where's that old tom-cat?
"I said, where's that old tom-cat?"
He's a-gettin' high when he winked one eye
And he says (hic) "Hey buddy where's that old tom-cat?
Spoken: "I can lick him and his brother."

The old tom-cat come a slippin' in
Dashed over to the middle 'a' the floor,
The cat jumped over and the rat got sober
And he never got drunk no more.

CHORUS:
He didn't get drunk no more
No he never got drunk no more
The cat jumped over and the rat got sober
(poor little feller)
And he never got drunk no more.

BLACKBERRY RAG

I composed this tune after listening to Texas fiddlers do things like *Beaumont Rag* and *Smoky Mountain Rag*. I came up with a different tune, and I called it *Blackberry Rag*. At first I thought that I had probably heard it somewhere before, but after I got to thinking about old-time fiddle tunes, I decided it really was a new one.

BLACKBERRY RAG

Flat-Pick/Capo 2nd Fret

By Arthel "Doc" Watson

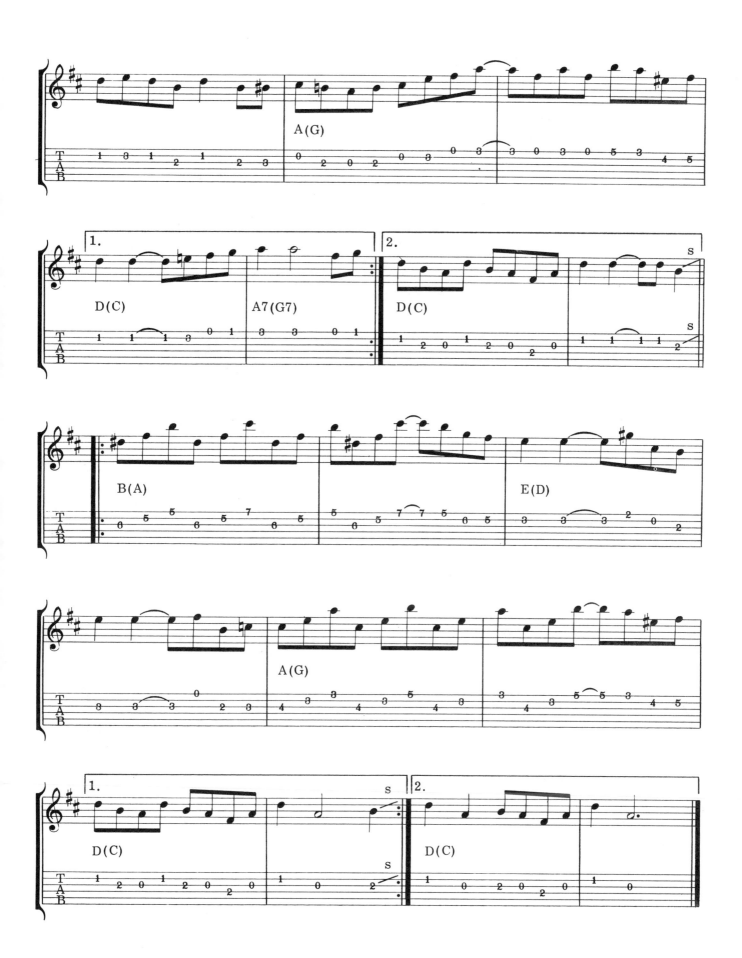

SETTIN' ON TOP OF THE WORLD

The first version I ever heard of *Settin' On Top Of The World* was done by a Negro blues and jug band named The Mississippi Sheiks. I fashioned my arrangement from Frank Hutchinson's *The Train That Carried My Girl From Town* and *Worried Blues;* I just worked out a finger-picking version in an open tuning.

Sometimes when I sing the song I think of my guitar and how pretty it sounds, if I've got it in good tune, and the strings are good. Sometimes, I'm just living the part of that old boy whose woman has run off and left him. He may have been a little wayward, but he has been doing his best for her. He wants her to come back, but he isn't about to let her come back—he's bragging, sour grapes kind of bragging. He's sitting on top of the world, but he's so lonesome that he can hardly stand it without her.

D tuning: D A D F♯ A D/Finger-Pick/Capo 1st Fret

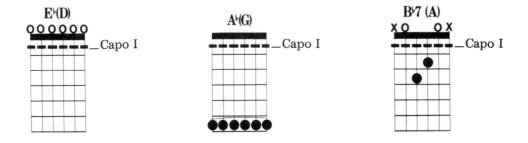

SETTIN' ON TOP OF THE WORLD

Arranged and adapted by A. Doc Watson

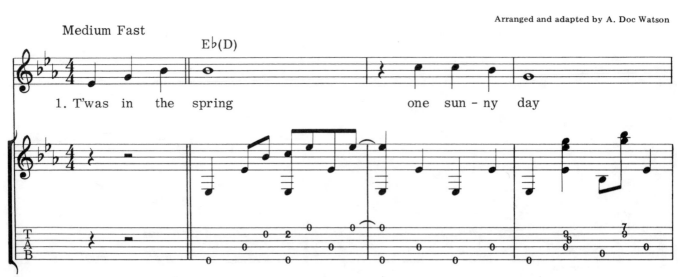

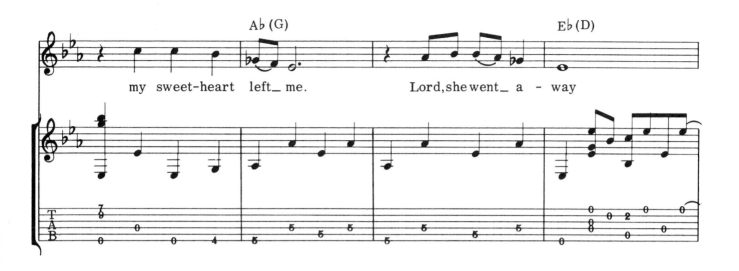

my sweet-heart left_ me. Lord, she went_ a - way

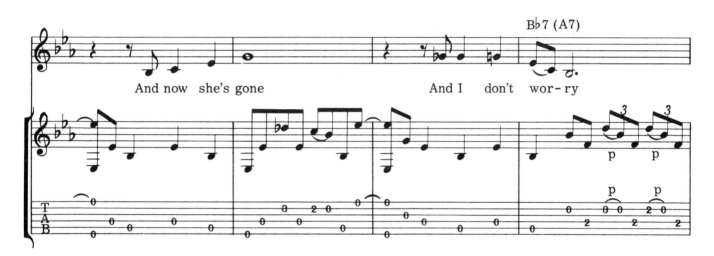

And now she's gone And I don't wor-ry

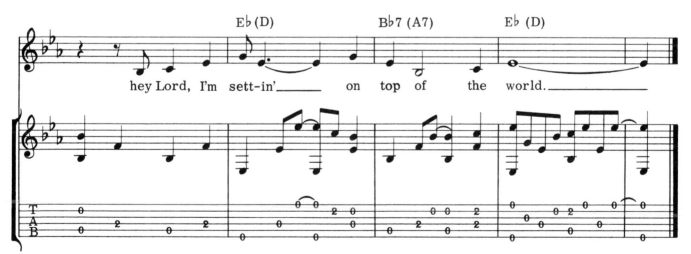

hey Lord, I'm sett-in'_____ on top of the world._____

She called me up	If you don't like my peaches	And don't you come here runnin'
From down in El Paso	Don't you shake my tree	Holding out your hand
She said, "Come back daddy	And get out of my orchard	I'm gonna get me a woman
Ooh-I need you so."	Let my peaches be.	Like you got your man.
And now she's gone, etc.	And now she's gone, etc.	And now she's gone, etc.

Repeat First Verse

SETTIN' ON TOP OF THE WORLD – Guitar Break

D tuning: D A D F# A D/ Finger-pick/Capo at 1st Fret

DON'T LET YOUR DEAL GO DOWN

Charlie Poole might turn over in his grave if he heard the way Merle and I do this song, which I heard him do years ago on record. We've speeded it up quite a bit.

It's a typical song of a fellow needing some money to give his girl friend some nice things that she doesn't have, and he's going off to the place where there's plenty of work. He tells her not to let the deal go down until he gets back. When he comes back, though, he finds that deal done fell down, you know, it done went down. She's got a dress on that the railroad man bought her and some pretty shoes that the mule driver in the mine bought her.

DON'T LET YOUR DEAL GO DOWN

Arranged and adapted by A. Doc Watson

I've been all a-round this whole wide world way down in Mem-phis Ten-nes - see. A-ny old place I hang my hat seems like home to me. Don't let your deal go down. Don't let your deal go down.. Don't let your deal go down sweet ma - ma for my last old dol - lar's gone.

Basic Accompaniment Pattern

Flat-Pick

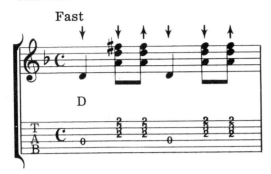

When I left my love behind
She's standin' in the door
She throwed her little arms
Around my neck and said,
"Sweet daddy please don't go."

Chorus

Now its who's gonna shoe your pretty
     little feet
Who's gonna glove your hand
And who's gonna kiss your ruby lips
Honey, who's gonna be your man?

She says Papa will shoe my pretty
     little feet
Mama will glove my hand
You can kiss my rosy lips
When you get back again.

Chorus

Where did you get them high-heel
     shoes
And that dress you wear so fine?
Got my shoes from a railroad man
Dress from a driver in the mine.

Chorus

DON'T LET YOUR DEAL GO DOWN – Guitar Break

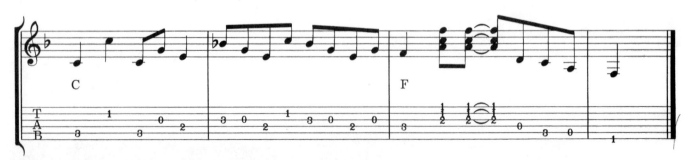

OPEN UP THEM PEARLY GATES

Open Up Them Pearly Gates is a song that I learned from a recording that Charlie and Bill Monroe did together on guitar and mandolin. In my mind I picture an old Baptist preacher who is also a singer. He has a very worldly congregation, or at least a few of them are. I won't say the whole bunch of them are so worldly, but there are a few rascals he likes very much as people, but he wants them to straighten out. He decides the best way to get them to listen is to put a little humor in his teaching. He tells them that all the chickens they've been stealing and all that drinking they've been doing on the gin pot won't make the good Lord look too kindly on them when the day comes.

OPEN UP THEM PEARLY GATES

Arranged and adapted by A. Doc Watson

Now lis-ten all you sin-ners If you want to go to heav-en, heav-en, you bet-ter get right down on your knees and pray. All you gam-blin' sin-ners you'd bet-ter quit say-in' sev-en 'lev-en you'd bet-ter get read-y for to meet that judg-ment day.

Chorus

O-pen up them pearl-y gates, O-pen up them pearl-y gates, O-pen up them pearl-y gates for me.

When you hear that trum-pet blast, I'll be com-in' home at last, O-pen up them pearl-y gates for me.

Basic Accompaniment Pattern

Carter Style with Flat-Pick/Capo 3rd Fret

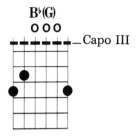

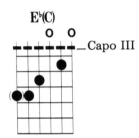

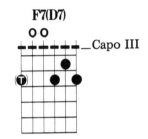

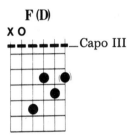

I've done had a vision
I've seen them pearly gates close
And then I seen you sinners all outside
You'd better make your decision
And pray that you'll be chosen, chosen,
It'll be too late when you lay down and die.

Chorus

Better go out to your chicken roost
And ask yourself an honest question
And the good Lord's gonna know it if you lie
You'd better turn all them chickens loose
Or you're gonna die from indigestion
When you eat that stolen chicken pie.

Chorus

You'd better take that old keg of gin
And dump it every bit right in the river
And don't you let old Satan stay your hand
For if you fill it up again
It's a gonna eat a hole right in your liver
And the gates won't open when you
    reach that promised land.

Chorus

OPEN UP THEM PEARLY GATES - Guitar Break

FAIR MAID IN THE GARDEN

This version of *The Fair Maid In The Garden* I learned from Stewart Yonce, a gent I think a lot of. He really liked this song, and it is his melody that I use. The words, however, I learned from Dolly Greer.

I can live the song as I sing it. It's just about a boy who pictures himself in the position of the guy who comes back home and finds that sweet and true girl who waited for him.

FAIR MAID IN THE GARDEN

Arranged and adapted by A. Doc Watson

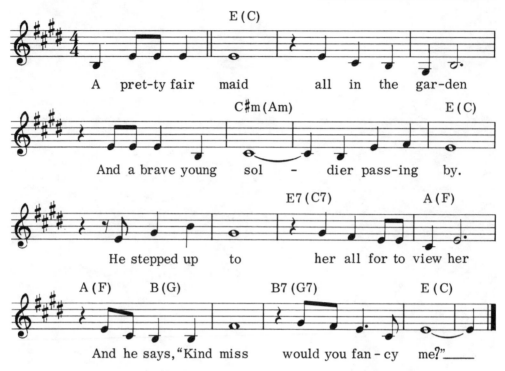

A pret-ty fair maid all in the gar-den
And a brave young sol - dier pass-ing by.
He stepped up to her all for to view her
And he says, "Kind miss would you fan-cy me?"____

I've traveled through many foreign
  countries
I've seen their queens and ladies fine
But I've never beheld such heavenly
  beauty
Would you be my lover, let me call you
  mine.

You're not the man I'll give the honor
You're not the man that I took you to be
Or you wouldn't impose on a single lady
Who's not your bride, and she never can be.

For I have a true love in the army
Seven years ago he crossed the sea
And if he stays there seven years longer
No man on earth will marry me.

Perhaps your true love has been
  drown-ded
He may lie on some battlefield slain
Or if he's taken some fine girl to marry
Then you'll never see his face again.

Oh yes, my true love may be drown-ded
Perhaps he's on some battlefield slain
But if he's taken some fine girl to marry
Then I love the girl that's married him.

He pulled his hand all out of his pockets
His fingers being so long and slim
She spied the gold ring on his finger
The some gold ring she had given him.

She fell into his arms a weepin'
And he gave her kisses, one, two, three
Saying don't you remember your jolly
  soldier
He's now returned to marry thee.

Basic Accompaniment Pattern

Finger-Pick/Capo 4th Fret

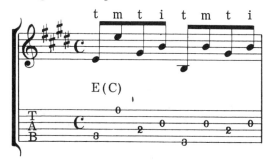

E (C)

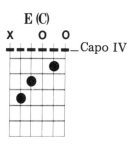

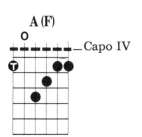

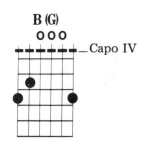

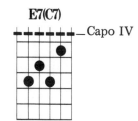

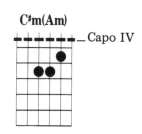

FAIR MAID IN THE GARDEN − Guitar Break

THE LONE PILGRIM

We are back to the good, old-time music again. This is one of the old songs that I've heard just as long as I can remember. My father, who was named General Watson, was the singing leader in our little country church, and *The Lone Pilgrim* was his favorite song.

When I think of this hymn I remember something that happened when Dad was leading the singing. Whenever he got a frog in his throat or missed a note to cough, the whole congregation had to stop singing until Dad could start up again. Once, the congregation was singing along, but Dad coughed, so everyone stopped except for a lady with a real high-pitched voice. She didn't realize that everyone had stopped singing, so she just stuck up there on a high note. Everybody was giggling, and the service was just about ruined, but Dad just finished coughing and started the congregation up singing again. You could hear a trace of a chuckle in his voice, though.

Basic Accompaniment Pattern

Flat-Pick or Thumb-Strum

THE LONE PILGRIM

Arranged and adapted by A. Doc Watson

I _____ came _____ to the place in the
lone _____ pil-grim way_____ and _____ pen-sive-ly
stood by his tomb when _____ in _____ a low
whis - per, I heard _____ some-thing say, _____ How_____
sweet - ly I sleep here a - lone.

The tempest may howl
And the loud thunder roar
And gathering storms may arise
But calm is my feeling
And rested my soul
The tears are all wiped from my eyes.

The call from my master
Compelled me from home
No kindred or relatives nigh
I met the contagion
And sank to the tomb
My soul flew to mansions on high.

Go tell my companion
And children most dear
To weep not for me now I'm gone
The same that hath led me through
    scenes most severe
Has kindly assisted me on.

PHARAOH

Pharaoh is a song which I composed eighteen years ago. I was sitting on the porch at my mother's, and my daughter, Nancy, was a little baby then. The pharaoh locusts were up around the house there on the mountain, but there were only a few of them. One of those little rascals, a male, come up in a little bush out there in the yard and he said, "Wheeeeooooh." He'd wait about sixty seconds or a half a minute maybe, and he'd do it again. I got to thinking, why doesn't somebody write a song about old Pharaoh and the plague. The people who study insects say that the pharaoh locusts have nothing to do with the Pharaoh's plague, but I'm not inclined to agree. *Pharaoh* was written out of pure inspiration from the story of Pharaoh and how the plagues tormented him because he wouldn't free the children of Israel from bondage.

Basic Accompaniment Pattern

Flat-Pick, thumb
or hand-strum/Capo 3rd Fret

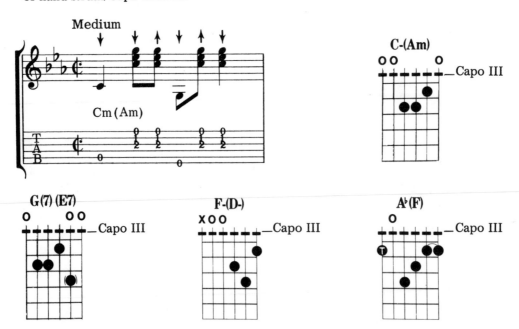

96

PHARAOH

Composed, Words and Music by A. Doc Watson

A long time a-go in the land of E - gypt
Chil - dren of Is - rael were bound, They were
slaves in the land of Phar - aoh mak - in'
bricks and a till-ing the ground. Then the
Lord sent Mo - ses to Phar-aoh. He said,
"Phar-aoh, you're to blame for all the plague that's com - in'
on your land and the lo - cust gon - na cry__ your
name, yeah." "Phar - aoh,__ Phar - aoh,__ the
lo - cust gon - na cry__ your name."

Then Moses said to Pharaoh
"Pharaoh you should know
"Our God will turn his wrath upon you
"If you don't let his people go.

CHORUS
"Pharaoh, Pharaoh
"You must let my people go."

Well, the flies got so thick
Way down in Egypt
The people couldn't eat for them
And the frogs came and got into old Pharaoh's house
They were sent for to torment him.

Then the darkness got so thick they could feel it
Because he disobeyed God
The hailstones fell that weighed a ton
And the streams all turned to blood.

CHORUS
"Pharaoh, Pharaoh,"
The locusts still cried his name.

God told his servant Moses
"My people must be led
"Out of Egypt by the way—the wilderness
"And across a sea called Red."

The Lord made a way through the middle of the sea
And when all his children walked through
Old Pharaoh defied the Lord and said "Now,
"That's the way we'll cross too."

Well, he marched horses on the bottom of the sea
His chariots and horses and men
Then the good Lord destroyed them all at one time
He rolled the waters together again.

CHORUS:
"Pharaoh, Pharaoh"
The locusts still cry his name.

DILL PICKLE RAG

Bill Hopkins, one of the original members of Al Hopkins' Bucklebusters, taught me *Dill Pickle Rag.* He was the group's pianist, and he did some fine ragtime piano work. He really loved this song, and the first time he played it for me, he must have seen my ears perk up like a hound's ears because he said, "Boy, you could learn to play that on the guitar, I bet five dollars." I have come up with a condensed and half complete version of the tune—I can't claim that it's all there. Merle can play it on the banjo so that it sounds a lot more like the way old Bill Hopkins played it.

DILL PICKLE RAG

Flat-Pick

Arranged and adapted by A. Doc Watson

Fast

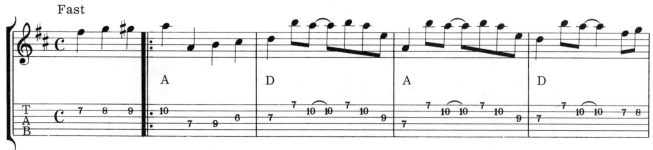

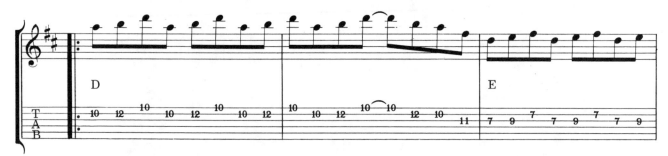

DOWN IN THE VALLEY TO PRAY

This is a whole different picture in music. One thing it brings to mind is my grandmother singing those old songs as she went about doing her work. In the church they'd get the whole congregation in on those songs, and there was some spirit there. Some people say it was just the spirit of togetherness, but I think it was the spirit of God. They sang a harmony to it that was beautiful—usually three parts, with quite a few members of the congregation taking up each part. Boy, it was really pretty.

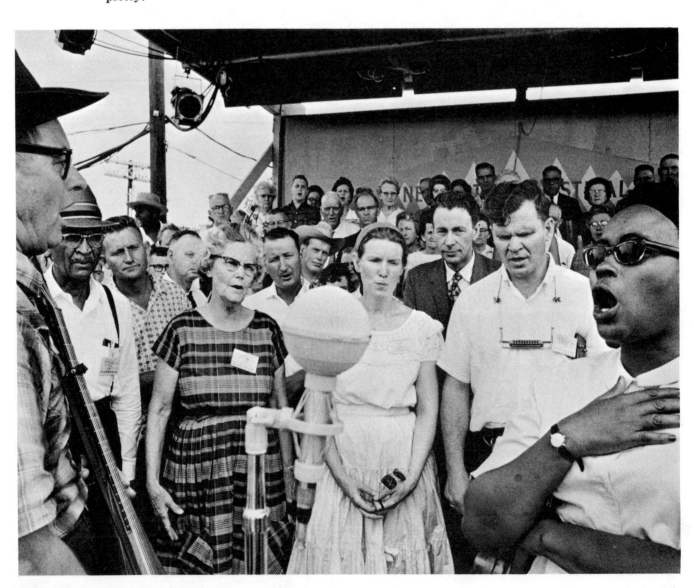

DOWN IN THE VALLEY TO PRAY

Unaccompanied Voice

Medium

Arranged and adapted by A. Doc Watson

As I went Down In The Val-ley To Pray stu-dy-in' a-bout that good old way and who shall wear the star-ry crown good Lord ___ show me the way.

Fine

Oh fa - thers let's go down ___

Let's go ___ down come on down, ___ Oh fa - thers

D. C. al Fine

let's go down ___ Down In The Val-ley To Pray.

As I went down in the valley to pray
Studyin' about that good old way
And who shall wear the robe and
  crown
Good Lord, show me the way.
Oh mothers let's go down,
Come on down don't you wanna go
  down?
Come on mothers and let's go down,
Down in the valley to pray.

. . . Oh brothers (similarly)

As I went down in the valley to pray
Studyin' about the good old way
And who shall wear the robe and
  crown
Good Lord, show me the way.
Come on sinners and let's go down,
Let's go down, oh come on down,
Come on sinners and let's go down,
Down in the valley to pray.

Repeat First Verse

RISIN' SUN BLUES

Now we get back to a good old friend of mine, the late Clarence Ashley, who was to me one of the greats in old-time country music. This is not his arrangement exactly, but it is influenced ninety-five percent by his arrangement.

Basic Accompaniment Pattern

Flat-Pick/All strings tuned down
one full step: E to D; B to A; etc.

D (E)

G (A)

A7(B7)

RISIN' SUN BLUES

Arranged and adapted by A. Doc Watson

1. There is a — house down in New Or -
leans They call the Ris - ing — Sun ——— And it's
been — the ru - in of a man - y poor
boy And me, — Oh God, — for one. ———

Then fill the glasses to the brim
Let the drinks go merrily around
And we'll drink to the health of a
   rounder (poor boy)
Who goes from town to town.

The only thing that a rounder needs
Is his suitcase and a trunk
And the only time he's satisfied
Is when he's on a drunk.

Now boys don't believe what a girl
   tells you
Though her eyes be blue or brown
Unless she's on some scaffold high
Saying, "Boys, I can't come down."

Go tell my youngest brother
Not to do the things I've done
But to shun that house down in New
   Orleans
They call the Rising Sun.

I'm goin' back, back to New Orleans
For my race is nearly run
Gonna spend the rest of my wicked
   life
Beneath that Rising Sun.

RISIN' SUN BLUES – Guitar Break

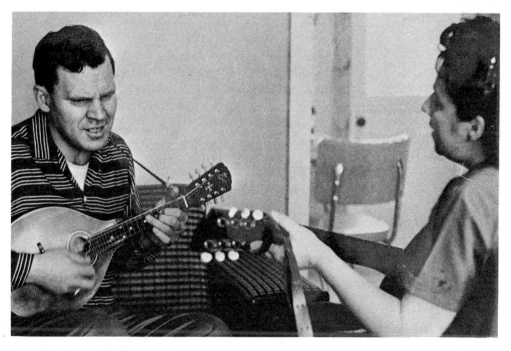

YOUR LONE JOURNEY

Your Lone Journey is a song that my wife, Rosa Lee, and I composed. I was fooling around with the guitar one morning when Rosa Lee was sweeping the house, and I came up with parts of the tune. I was inspired partly by the pretty melody of *Pretty Saro*, and the tune is also reminiscent of Irish and Scottish sounding things from the old days. We got to thinking about how awful it would be if a person's mate had to leave; it was mainly Rosa Lee that put our feelings into the verses.

YOUR LONE JOURNEY

Words and Music by Rosa Lee Watson and A. Doc Watson

God's __ giv-en us __ years of __
hap-pi-ness here, __ Now __ we must part
and __ as the __ an-gels __ come and __
call for you the __ pains of grief __ tug __
at my heart. Oh, my dar-ling,
my __ dar-ling, My heart
breaks as you take __ your __ lone jour-ney.

Oh the days will be empty
The nights so long
Without you my love,
And as God calls for you
I'm left alone
But we will meet
In heaven above.

Fond memories I'll keep
Of the happy days,
That on earth we've trod
And when I come
We will walk hand in hand
As one in Heaven
In the family of God.

Chorus

Basic Accompaniment Pattern

Play Carter Style: the thumb picks the bass notes while the index and middle fingers "brush" the top notes of the chord.

YOUR LONE JOURNEY – Guitar Break

WE SHALL ALL BE REUNITED

I learned this song from a recording in my dad's collection. A blind man from Kentucky, Alfred Karnes, did *We Shall All Be Reunited* as well as seven other sides for Brunswick. I love it because it is typical of the old-time Baptist singing, and it expresses the way I would feel if all of my family went into the Beyond and I were still here. I sing it because I love it for what it is.

Basic Accompaniment Pattern

Play Carter Style: the thumb picks the bass notes while the index and middle fingers "brush" the top strings up and down.

WE SHALL ALL BE REUNITED

Arranged and adapted by A. Doc Watson

Verse:

1. Where is now my fa-ther's fam-'ly?
They were here so long a-go,
Seat-ed round the old home fire-side
Bright-ened by the rud-died glow.

Chorus:

We shall all be re-u-ni-ted
In that land be-yond the skies,
Where there'll be no sep-a-ra-tions,
No more part-ings, no more sighs.

Some have gone to lands far distant
And with others made their home
Some upon the earth have wandered
All their lives have chose to roam.

Chorus

Some have gone from us forever
For with us they could not stay
They have all dispersed and wandered
Gone away, so far away.

We shall meet beyond the river
In that land of pure delight
Without sickness or our sorrows
We'll have joys ever bright.

Chorus

ST. JAMES HOSPITAL

I first heard this ballad from a record by Pete Seeger, *American Folk Songs and Ballads.* By reading the notes, I found out that John Lomax collected the song from Iron Head Baker back in the thirties.

As I sing this song, I can just picture that as I'm walking along, I pass by a hospital, but it's really nothing much more than a place to put sick people. I look through the window and I see an old cowboy lying on a bed; he looks so pitiful in his dying condition that I feel that I have to go in and give him a word of comfort. He is in the grip of death, and he asks me to go get the preacher for him. He wants me to get some pretty girls to come to the funeral and cover his body with roses. I really live this song as I sing it.

Basic Accompaniment Pattern

Capo 2nd Fret/Rapid and fluid arpeggiation: the ring finger of the right hand (a) plays the top note; the middle finger (m) plays the next highest note; and the index finger (i) plays the lowest of the three notes; the thumb plays a bass note on the 1st beat of each new chord change or whatever else feels appropriate.

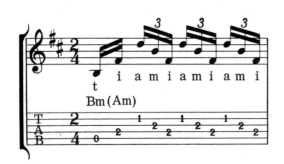

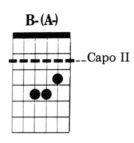

B- (A-)

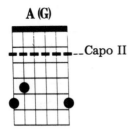

A (G)

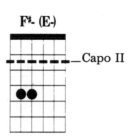

F#- (E-)

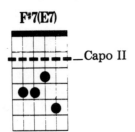

F#7(E7)

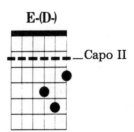

E-(D-)

ST. JAMES HOSPITAL

Arranged and adapted by A. Doc Watson

"Sit ye down by me
And hear my sad story
Sit ye down by me
And sing me a song
For my poor head is achin'
And my sad heart is breakin'
I'm a poor cowboy
That know'd he done wrong.

"Send for that doctor
To come and heal up my body
And send for the preacher
To come and pray for my soul
For my poor head is achin'
And my sad heart is breakin'
I'm a poor cowboy
And hell is my dole.

Get 16 pretty maidens
To come and carry my coffin
16 pretty maidens
To come and sing me a song
And tell 'em to bring some 'a' them
Sweet smellin' roses
So they can smell me
As they tote me along.

Beat the drum slowly
And play the pipe lowly
Play the Death March
As ye carry me along
Throw bunches of lilies
All over my coffin
There goes a poor cowboy
That know'd he done wrong.

PRETTY SARO

I learned the pretty melody and most of the words to *Pretty Saro* from my pappy-in-law again, Gaither Carlton. Two of the verses I learned from Dolly Greer. I never could get an exact imitation of that beautiful little lope that Gaither gets on the banjo, so I decided to do the song unaccompanied.

This song makes me realize the way I would feel if I had to leave Rosa Lee for a long time; I'd have the exact sort of feeling as the guy who wrote *Pretty Saro* a long time ago.

PRETTY SARO

Arranged and adapted by A. Doc Watson

Pretty Saro, Pretty Saro,
Likewise my mother too
I have started for to ramble
This country all through,
And when I get tired
I'll sit down and weep
And I'll think of my Pretty Saro
Wherever I sleep.

Oh it's not this lone journey
I'm a-dreadin' for to go
Not the country I believe in
And the debts that I owe,
But there's one thing that grieves me
And troubles my mind
It's a-leavin' my little darling
Way back here behind.

If I was a poet
And could write a fine hand
I would write my love a letter
That she'd long understand,
I would send it by the waters
Where the islands overflow
I'll remember my Pretty Saro
Wherever I go.

FROGGY WENT A-COURTIN'

I first heard this song when my Mama used to sing it to me; she only sang a couple of verses, and I must admit that I picked a lot more verses up from other sources.

This is the children's version of a much older song that dates back to the times of Queen Elizabeth. I imagine the original words of *Froggy Went A-Courtin'* made the song not quite a children's song.

Incidentally, there's another arrangement of this song which my daughter, Nancy, Rosa Lee and I, all sing harmony on.

FROGGY WENT A-COURTIN'

Arranged and adapted by A. Doc Watson

Frog-gy went a-court-in' and he did ride uh huh,_____ Frog-gy went a-court-in' and he did ride uh huh,_____ Frog-gy went a-court-in' and he did ride a sword and a pis-tol by his side uh huh._____

He rode right up to Miss Mousie's door, uh huh (2X)
He rode right up to Miss Mousie's door
And he hit it so hard he made it roar, uh huh.

Then Miss Mousie let him in, uh huh (2X)
Then Miss Mousie let him in
And the way they courted it was a sin, uh huh.

He took Miss Mousie right on his knee, uh huh (2X)
He took Miss Mousie right on his knee
And says Miss Mousie will you marry me, uh huh.

Miss Mousie says I don't know about that, uh huh (2X)
Miss Mousie says I don't know about that
But I believe to my soul you have to ask Uncle Rat, uh huh.

The old rat laughed as he gave away the bride, uh huh (2X)
The old rat laughed as he gave away the bride
He laughed and he laughed and he shook his fat sides, uh huh.

Where will the weddin' supper be, uh huh (2X)
Where will the weddin' supper be
Away down yonder in a holla tree, uh huh.

What did he get for the weddin' gown, uh huh (2X)
What did he get for the weddin' gown
A piece of hide of an old white houn', uh huh.

What will the weddin' supper be, uh huh (2X)
What will the weddin' supper be
Two butterbeans and a black-eyed pea, uh huh.

The first to come in was a big June bug, uh huh (2X)
The first to come in was a big June bug
A-dancin' around with a half pint jug, uh huh.

The second one in was a bumblebee, uh huh (2X)
The second one in was a bumblebee
A-dancin' around with a fiddle on his knee, uh huh.

The third man in was a little grey mouse, uh huh (2X)
The third man in was a little grey mouse
And he says Mr. Froggy could I rent you a house? uh huh.

Froggy went a-travelin' across the lake, uh huh (2X)
Froggy went a-travelin' across the lake
And he got swallowed up by a big black snake, uh huh.

FROGGY WENT A-COURTIN' – Banjo Break

Key of C [Tuning: $\begin{smallmatrix}5 & 4 & 3 & 2 & 1\\ g & C & G & \underline{B} & D\end{smallmatrix}$]

GEORGIE BUCK

When I think of this song, I remember my dad sitting on the porch after he'd made me a little fretless five-string. He picked up the banjo, and he started picking the tune and told me that it was called *Georgie Buck*. He sang a few words, and after he played the song a couple more times, I got enough of it together that I could pick it along on the banjo. It's about a fellow who was having some hard luck in his life, an old boy in trouble who had a woman who wasn't treating him right. It's always the kind of song I like to do if I'm feeling low, you know, sort of a bluesy thing, and yet, when you hear it on the banjo, there's another sound—a "things-will-be-all right-tomorrow" sound.

GEORGIE BUCK

Arranged & adapted by A.D. Watson

1. My name is Geor-gie Buck   Nev-er had no luck   Al - ways _____ been treat-ed this - a way,   Boys; _   Al - ways   been

treat-ed   this - a   way.   Oh

m   m   m h m t   m   m t m p m t   m   m t m p m t   m   m t m p m t

me____   and   it's   oh _____   my

m p m t m p m t   m   m t m   p m t   m   m t m h m t

what's goin'   to be - come___   of ____   me. _____

m d m t m p m t   m   m   m h m t   m   m t m p m t   m

Georgie Buck is dead
As he laid on his bed
He said, "Never let your woman
"Have her way boys,
"Never let your woman have her way.
"If you let her have her way
"She's gonna lead you astray
"Never let your woman have her way."

Repeat First Verse

Georgie Buck is dead
The last words he said was,
"Dig me a hole in the ground boys,
"Dig me a hole in the ground.
"Oh, me, and it's, oh, my
"What's gonna become of me,
"What's gonna become of me?"

GEORGIE BUCK - Banjo Break

Banjo tuning: GGDGBD Two-finger "Scruggs Style"

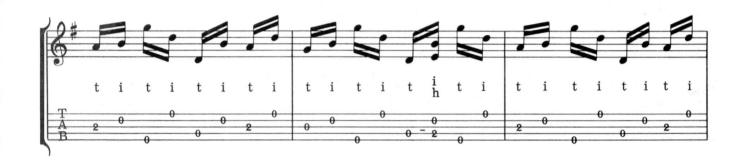

KATIE MORY

Bless my mother's heart, I've heard her sing this song ever since I was two or three years old. It's one of those fun songs about courting—about a fellow who wants to get just a little pushy (fresh) with a girl. The old boy gets her to go along down this beautiful path on the pretense that the plums are ripe and the grapes are good to eat. The girl realizes what it's all about, and she plays along to a certain point. She squeezes his hand, you know, to give him a little encouragement, and says, "You climb up that tree and see if Mama is near, and if she's not, we'll just go over to this here grove and have a real good time." Boy, when she gets him up that tree, she laughs and makes a fool out of him. She says, "You look like an owl. I despise you, you rascal," and turns around and runs right back to the house.

That's just exactly the way some of the girls were: they were coy with their virtues and took care of themselves, but they did it in a way that the guy really respected. After the fellow thinks about it, after he gets over his little anger, he thinks, "God, she's really nice, and the next time I make a play it will be in a decent way. I'd like to have that gal for my wife."

KATIE MORY

Adapted and Arranged by Arthel "Doc" Watson

Come all you fel - las from far and near
lis - ten to my sto - ry gon - na
tell you 'bout the plan I made to
fool Miss Ka - tie Mo - ry too da
rod - dle neck ee eye ay rye - o.

I went down to Miss Katie's house just like some clever feller,
And I told her that the plums and grapes is a-gettin' ripe and meller.

Chorus (too-da-rah-etc.)

I told her that her sister Nan that lived in yander's holler,
Had sent for her to come down there and stay one half an hour.

Chorus

As we was walkin' through the field she squeezed my hand the fiercer,
Said mama has come this way and she will catch us here sir.

Chorus

If you will climb up yander's tree and see if she is near sir,
Then we'll go to that pretty grove and court and sport an hour.

Chorus

Oh how he heaved to climb that tree till he was nearly winded,
And Miss Katie stood and smiled, and watched to see how high he ascended.

Chorus

His heart was a-thumpin' in his breast, the tree was gently swayin',
As he looked down Miss Katie smiled and he heard what she was sayin'.

Chorus

Your ugly looks I do despise, you look just like an owl sir,
You scratched down like you scratched up for I'm a-goin' home sir.

Chorus

KATIE MORY - Banjo Break

Key of C minor   Tuning: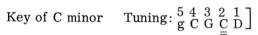

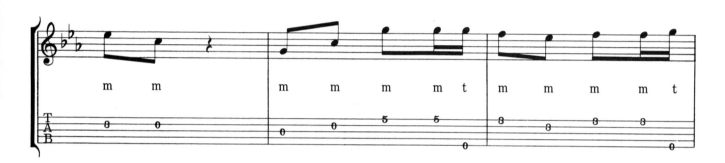

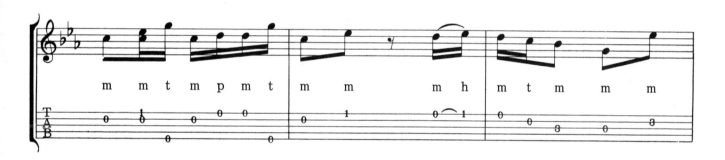

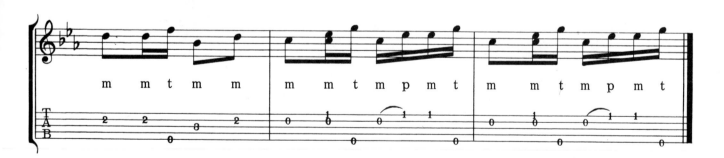

Discography

The following is a list of all of Doc's songs presented in this book which are available on Vanguard records:

Georgie Buck: . . . . *Doc Watson VRS-9152*
VSD-79152

Tom Dooley: . . . . *Doc Watson VRS-9152*
VSD-79152

Doc's Guitar: . . . . *Doc Watson VRS-9152*
VSD-79152
Country Music and Bluegrass at Newport VRS-9146
VSD-79146
Doc Watson, On Stage VSD-9/10

Black Mountain Rag: . . . . . . *Doc Watson VRS-9152*
VSD-79152
Country Music and Bluegrass at Newport VRS-9146
VSD-79146

The Train That Carried
My Girl From Town: . . . . . . *Doc Watson In Nashville, Good Deal VSD-79276*

Deep River Blues: . . . . *Doc Watson VRS-9152*
VSD-79152
Doc Watson, On Stage VSD-9/10
The Sound of Folk Music, Volume III SRV-140
SRV-140 F.D.

Omie Wise: . . . . *Doc Watson VRS-9152*
VSD-79152

The Old Man Below: . . . . . . *Doc Watson, Home Again! VRS-9239*
VSD-79239

Matty Groves: . . . . *Doc Watson, Home Again! VRS-9239*
VSD-79239

Southbound: . . . . *Doc Watson, Southbound VRS-9213*
VSD-79213
Doc Watson, On Stage VSD-9/10

A-Rovin' On A Winter's Night: *Doc Watson, Home Again! VRS-9239*
VSD-79239

Georgie: . . . . *Doc Watson, Home Again! VRS-9239*
VSD-79239

Katie Mory: . . . . *Doc Watson, Home Again! VRS-9239*
VSD-79239

The Call Of The Road: . . . . *Doc Watson, Southbound VRS-9213*
VSD-79213

F.F.V.: . . . . *Doc Watson, Home Again! VRS-9239*
VSD-79239

Blackberry Rag: . . . . *Doc Watson In Nashville, Good Deal VSD-79276*

Nothing To It: . . . . *Doc Watson, Southbound VRS-9213*
VSD-79213

The Intoxicated Rat: . . . . . *Doc Watson VRS-9152*
VSD-79152

Spike Driver's Blues: . . . . . . *Doc Watson, On Stage VSD-9/10*

Shady Grove: . . . . *Doc Watson In Nashville, Good Deal VSD-79276*

Down In The Valley To Pray: *Doc Watson, Home Again! VRS-9239*
VSD-79239

Open Up Them Pearly Gates: *Doc Watson, On Stage VSD-9/10*

Don't Let Your Deal Go Down: *Doc Watson, On Stage VSD-9/10*

Settin' On Top Of The World: *Doc Watson VRS-9152*
VSD-79152

St. James Hospital: . . . . *Doc Watson VRS-9152*
VSD-79152

Dill Pickle Rag: . . . . *Doc Watson, Home Again! VRS-9239*
VSD-79239

Froggy Went A-Courtin' . . . . *Doc Watson, Home Again! VRS-9239*
VSD-79239

Pretty Saro: . . . . *Doc Watson, Home Again!* VRS-9239
                                                      VSD-79239

Risin' Sun Blues: . . . . *Doc Watson And Son* VRS-9170
                                                      VSD-79170

We Shall All Be Reunited: . . . *Doc Watson And Son* VRS-9170
                                                      VSD-79170

As of May, 1971 the following songs in this book have not been recorded by Doc:
Lovin' Emma
Fair Maid In The Garden
The Lone Pilgrim
Pharaoh
Your Lone Journey

In addition to the above albums for Vanguard, Doc has also cut:

Old Time Music at Newport VRS-9147
                                                      VSD-79147

Traditional Music at Newport 1961 Part I VRS-9182
                                                      VSD-79182

Newport Folk Festival 1964 Evening Concerts Vol. III VRS-9186
                                                      VSD-79186

Tapes from Doc's recordings on Vanguard are available through:

Ampex Corporation
2201 Lunt Avenue
Elk Grove Village, Illinois 60007